THE GEORGIAN AND REGENCY LEGACY

THE BUILDINGS OF SHROPSHIRE

Volume 3

THE GEORGIAN AND REGENCY LEGACY

1730-1840

Lawrence Garner

First published in the UK in 1990 by
Swan Hill Press, an imprint of
Airlife Publishing Ltd.

British Library Cataloguing in Publication Data

Garner, Lawrence
The Georgian legacy — (The buildings of Shropshire V. 3).
1. Shropshire, architecture history
I. Title II. Series
720.94245

ISBN 1 85310 129 X

Swan Hill Press

An Imprint of Airlife Publishing Ltd.

101 Longden Road, Shrewsbury SY3 9EB, England.

Contents

Preface

The Buildings of Shropshire *Series*

During the last twenty years there has been a remarkable upsurge of interest in all aspects of the English landscape — archaeology, geography, natural history, architecture, industrial remains and anything else that enables us to build up a picture of local history on the ground. This interest has been accompanied by an unprecedented concern for conservation. But all too often the people who feel strongly that the best of the past should be preserved are diffident about their lack of specialist knowledge.

The *Buildings of Shropshire* series is an attempt to provide the general reader with an introduction to the man-made structures in the Shropshire landscape, from hill forts to industrial buildings, from stately homes to cottages. The emphasis is on how to look and where to look, so each fully-illustrated volume contains essential background information and practical guidance for those who want to get out and see for themselves. Jargon is kept to a minimum, but a glossary of technical terms is provided.

There is inevitably some overlap of material from one volume to another, and this applies particularly to the descriptions of building methods, which have changed far more slowly than architectural styles. Readers will perhaps excuse the repetition, which is inevitable if each volume is to be self-contained.

The series is planned in four volumes as follows:

1 – The Pre-16th century Legacy (from the Bronze Age to c. 1530)
2 – The Tudor and Stuart Legacy (from 1530 to 1730)
3 – The Georgian and Regency Legacy (from 1730 to 1840)
4 – The Victorian Legacy (from 1840 to 1914)

Introduction to Volume 3

In continuing the story of Shropshire's built landscape I have tried to follow the plan established in Volume 2, maintaining a balance between history and fieldwork. The period 1730-1840, however, saw two significant innovations — the influence of the professional architect and the development of a distinctive industrial landscape.

The history of architecture can be forbidding but can hardly be ignored in a series of this kind, so I have included an introductory section which attempts to explain in outline the national movements that ultimately affected Shropshire. The number of buildings directly inspired by architects was fairly small, but many more were the results of builders' pattern books, so a broad knowledge of architectural fashion is essential.

The development of a recognisable industrial region on the Shropshire coalfield was a complex process well beyond the scope of this book. Luckily the admirable series of inexpensive pamphlets produced by the Ironbridge Gorge Museum Trust has covered the ground in a very accessible way, and I have not thought it necessary to repeat the story here; the section on industry comprises mainly a gazetteer of the more important buildings and sites. On the other hand, the canal-building that followed the upsurge of industrial activity has not been chronicled so conveniently, so a brief history of the main developments is included, together with a gazetteer.

For reasons of space I have had to omit any study of Shropshire's roads during this period, but the subject will be taken up in the volume on the period 1840-1914, and will perhaps make more sense in the context of Victorian progress in road engineering.

It is a sign of the times that on several occasions I was refused permission to photograph country houses, so the book lacks some illustrations that would have been useful and instructive. In one or two cases it was made clear that for security reasons a study of the exterior, even without the camera, would be unwelcome. Most house-owners, however, accepted without protest my incursions into their privacy, and I thank them for their courtesy and interest.

In return, I undertook to make it clear that their houses are included purely as a record and not as an indication that casual visitors are welcome. Owners realise, of course, that people seriously interested in architecture may want to view their property, but *prior arrangement by letter or telephone is essential.* The vast majority of these houses are included in the gazetteer in Part Six and I have noted those that can be seen without intruding on private land.

Lawrence Garner

Part One
Progress in Architecture 1730-1840

The previous volume in this series was concerned almost entirely with houses and dealt with the remarkable upsurge of building during the sixteenth and seventeenth centuries. In this volume we have to look at a wider variety of structures in the landscape — houses certainly, but also new kinds of buildings associated with industry, agriculture, transport and public welfare. There is also another significant difference. Most of the buildings of the Tudor and Stuart period in Shropshire owed little to architectural dictates; they may have reflected an awareness of fashion, but they remained expressions of individual tastes and preferences. The Georgian period saw the arrival of the architect in Shropshire.

Architecture was a matter of vital interest among cultured people throughout Britain during the eighteenth and early nineteenth centuries; it was part of a general hankering after metropolitan fashion that affected even the remotest parts of the country. Improvements to roads enabled wealthy people to travel to the capital and see innovations in fashion for themselves. Better transport also led to the practice of extensive visiting of friends and relations in other parts of the country, and these journeys often included the viewing of notable new houses. In these ways the taste of a small number of London architects could achieve disproportionate influence throughout the nation.

One result of this universal interest was the proliferation of architectural pattern books. Sometimes these books represented the first-hand work of distinguished men, but more often the authors were talented draughtsmen who reproduced variations on current ideas in architecture and adapted them for a wide range of buildings. Whatever their source, the pattern books had the effect of imposing a uniformity of general design and of ensuring that even small houses reflected 'national' taste.

At first, of course, there was an inevitable time-lag of a decade or more between architectural developments in London and their appearance in a remote county like Shropshire. As the century progressed, however, this delay became shorter for two reasons. First, a few landowners in the county commissioned major architects like Sir Richard Chambers, James Wyatt, Robert Mylne, Sir John Soane and John Nash to build new mansions or to remodel older ones, thus provoking the desire for imitation. Secondly there emerged a group of local architects capable of grasping new fashions and adapting them to the tastes and pockets of the less wealthy.

These local men included, among others, Thomas Farnolls Pritchard, John Hiram Haycock and his son Edward, John Carline and John Tilley. Their names recur continually in the history of Shropshire building, and while they may not have been brilliant innovators they produced buildings of solid worth. George Steuart was another provincial architect who never achieved a

A typical small Georgian country house of three bays and two-and-a-half storeys. Houses like this, built from a pattern-book, are common throughout the county. The porch is Victorian.

national reputation in his lifetime but who features in the standard textbooks as the creator of Attingham Park and St Chad's church in Shrewsbury. Nor should we forget Thomas Telford, whose architectural talents were nurtured in Shropshire.

Telford, Carline and Tilley were stonemasons; Pritchard started out as a joiner, while the Haycocks no doubt considered themselves to be builders first and foremost — a reminder that the vast majority of Shropshire buildings of this period were designed and built in the old way, by craftsmen-builders who were handed a design from a pattern book and asked to produce something like it.

Taking all this into account, it is hardly surprising that the chief characteristic of the buildings of the later eighteenth and early nineteenth centuries is harmonious conformity extending through a remarkably wide range of structures. A new farmhouse could closely resemble a fashionable town residence, a canal warehouse could be built in the style of a town hall, and the architectural taste of a landowner would dictate the appearance of his estate cottages.

Georgian and Regency architecture is in fact more varied than many people think, but it is true to say that the period from 1730 to 1840 was dominated by styles which were variations on a few basic themes — Palladian, Picturesque, Greek Revival and so on. Given the wide application of a limited number of concepts it is fortunate that the buildings of the period continue to be admired and to be found universally acceptable in town and country. Indeed, it is often forgotten that architecture which is regarded as quintessentially English evolved from models which were totally foreign, and one result of the dominance of architects was the virtual loss of the intuitive native tradition that had found vigorous expression in the era of timber-framing.

It is evident that any local survey of the period must start with an outline of the changing patterns of national taste, and it will be necessary to recapitulate briefly part of the account contained in Volume 2.

The sudden expansion of building in the second half of the sixteenth century saw much use of the traditional timber or stone, but the important technical innovation of the early seventeenth century was the gradual acceptance of brick as a primary building material — a development of enormous significance that contributed more than anything else to the future appearance of our built landscape.

From the late sixteenth century onwards an awareness of 'Renaissance'

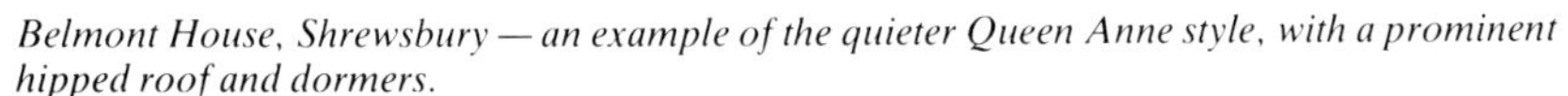

Belmont House, Shrewsbury — an example of the quieter Queen Anne style, with a prominent hipped roof and dormers.

style spread to the remoter counties from the more fashionable south and east of England. It originated in the rediscovery in fifteenth-century Italy of classical Roman design, resulting in greater emphasis on symmetry, proportion and rectangular forms, and also in the use of the classical 'Orders' of columns, pilasters and mouldings to embellish and 'articulate' the façade of a building.

The style was based on the ideas of the Italian architect Palladio, interpreted and introduced into England by Inigo Jones in the early years of the seventeenth century. Palladian architecture was more of a concept than a visual style, laying great emphasis on symmetry, geometrical proportion and the accurate use of Roman orders and embellishments. Jones's own work tended towards 'correctness' and the restrained use of external decoration, but, perhaps because of the political uncertainty of the period that followed, his designs did not lead immediately to a rash of imitations.

It was not until well after the Restoration in 1660 that a new group of innovative architects appeared, and the great impetus was the need to rebuild after the fire of London in 1666. The dominant figure was Sir Christopher Wren, who was not content to adopt Palladianism in the severe and restrained form demonstrated by Inigo Jones. He and contemporaries like Hawksmoor and Vanbrugh wanted freedom to express their own ideas within the broad rules of classicism, and this individual approach was to lead to what is usually called 'Baroque' style, which adopted all the elements of Palladianism but assembled them in flamboyant ways that Palladio would no doubt have shuddered at.

Well-known examples of Baroque style are Chatsworth, Castle Howard and Blenheim Palace, although the fashion was followed in a number of smaller country houses throughout England. What they have in common is symmetry, a rectangular theme (based on the great rectangle of the façade itself), very free proportions and a variety of embellishments in the form of pediments, columns, pilasters, parapets, cornices, balustrades and finials. They are intended to demonstrate magnificence, and are very different from Inigo Jones's chaste, classically correct structures.

These national developments infiltrated Shropshire in an uncertain and haphazard fashion. The county's early experimenters were reluctant to abandon traditional styles, so the first sign of Renaissance influence was usually a simple concern with symmetry, revealed in some timber-framed houses and in the twin gables of the seventeenth-century manor house. More daring experiments tended to result in a strange mixture of homely Englishness with classical embellishments, but after 1670 a fairly sophisticated interpretation of Renaissance principles began to appear in such houses as Longnor Hall, Bragginton Hall, Great Lyth, Halston Hall and Court of Hill. Cound Hall (1704) is generally reckoned to be the county's first full-blooded essay in Baroque, and it inspired several imitations associated with the builder Francis Smith of Warwick.

The distinctive Cound Hall style — red brick, hipped roofs, quoins, pilasters, eaves cornices and pediments, string courses, regular window patterns, enriched doorways and so on — is usually called 'provincial Baroque'. It is a rather derogatory term implying a naive and second-hand form of the self-indulgent architecture of Wren and his colleagues. Indeed,

Elaborate outbuildings reflecting the character of the house were a feature of the new country houses. This stable block is at Linley Hall (1742).

many landowners rejected its flamboyance, adapting the new ideas in the quieter and more elegant Queen Anne style. But there is no doubt that provincial Baroque houses, in town or country, made a powerful statement and marked out the owner as a man of wealth and fashion — much the same effect as that achieved earlier by lavishly-decorated timber-framing.

Apart from Cound Hall, other well-known Shropshire examples of provincial Baroque, built in the first thirty years of the eighteenth century, are Kinlet Hall, Buntingsdale, Mawley Hall, Davenport House, Berwick and Hardwick (Ellesmere). Urban versions of the style are exemplified by Hardwick House in Shrewsbury and Northgate House in Bridgnorth.

As the century progressed, however, there was a general trend in intellectual and artistic circles towards discipline and reason as expressed in scientific laws, mathematics and classical literature, and architecture did not escape this process. Inevitably there was a national reaction against the extravagance of Baroque style and a rediscovery of the cool correctness of the almost-forgotten Inigo Jones. Palladianism became the dominant architectural fashion of the first half of the eighteenth century.

The principles of Palladianism can be summed up as the correct observance of the practices of the 'ancients' (mainly Roman architects) and the strict application of fixed proportions. Thus Palladio had laid down seven ideal room proportions based on the circle and permutations of the cube; these in turn determined the proportions of the house. Embellishment was not banished, but it had to reflect accurately the classical usages, and especially

The central block of Attingham Hall. It is a neo-classical house of the 1780s, built in the severe Grecian taste which demanded ashlar stone and a giant portico.

the 'Orders' of columns and pilasters. Within these restrictions a surprising variety of architectural expression was possible.

Even when a reaction set in against pure Palladianism in the second half of the century it did not take the form of a break for freedom — architects either refined the rules or sought logical extensions of them.

There was, for example, a school of the Picturesque, a preoccupation with Nature, but it took a highly artificial form in which Nature was recreated in disciplined and acceptable ways. The landscaped parks of Capability Brown and his colleagues were an obvious consequence of this movement, but it also gave rise to a taste for quaintness and antiquity in architecture. Artificial ruins, Chinese temples. medieval summerhouses or thatched cottages (structures that we now call 'follies') sprang up on many estates. There was nothing frivolous about them. They served a serious purpose — to act as a reminder of the superiority of reason and modern civilised taste.

Another group of architects went in the opposite direction, taking the view that Palladianism had provided merely a second-hand version of classical style, and Roman style at that. One or two actually took themselves off to Greece to study original classical architecture at first hand, and their measurements and sketchbooks led to a new appreciation of the earliest Greek buildings. This movement, known as neo-classicism, laid emphasis on the Greek temple as the purest form of building, and it had a strong influence on public architecture in the early nineteenth century.

The important point about these and other mild experiments in the second half of the later Georgian period was not that they revolutionised architecture but that they indicated a relaxing of polite taste. When Palladianism was at its height a landowner might well wake in the night sweating with fear that his architect had miscalculated the dimensions of a pediment, thus provoking the ridicule of cultured men. By the end of the century a modest diversity of architecture was accepted, and one principle in particular was gaining ground — that the design of a building ought to be influenced by its function.

The success of 'Regency' architecture after 1800 was largely based on this idea, which made possible a new versatility among architects. It is best exemplified in the career of John Nash, who was capable of designing majestic London terraces, the fantastic Royal Pavilion at Brighton and a series of informal country villas in a variety of styles. The spa towns and new seaside resorts bear witness to the more relaxed approach that made it possible to describe buildings as 'charming' and even 'pretty' — a kind of vocabulary that could certainly not have been widely applied earlier in the eighteenth century.

Informal Regency architecture has a delicacy that sometimes approaches frivolity, and it is achieved by aiming for lightness and small scale rather than mass, and also by exploiting new materials and techniques. The use of ironwork in balconies and colonnades, for example, was a welcome relief

Millichope Hall illustrates the awareness of contrived landscaping which developed throughout the eighteenth century. The effect of the impressive Grecian portico is very striking.

The west lodge at Attingham Park, one of several examples of whimsical Gothick style to be found on the estate.

from the heaviness of brick and stone, while stucco rendering made exteriors rather less forbidding. This type of architecture is associated mainly with towns, but the early years of the nineteenth century saw the growing popularity of the small informal country villa as an alternative to the mansion.

Two other developments of the Regency period need to be mentioned. One was the 'Greek Revival', a consequence of the earnest neo-classicism described above. It produced severe country houses with massive porticos, and it was much in demand for public buildings in towns because it conferred reassuring solidity and respectability. The early banks used it freely. The other was a popular cult of the medieval, really an extension of Picturesque taste but perhaps given new impetus by the popular novels of Sir Walter Scott. The architectural result was a spate of 'Gothick' houses, either in a prettily quaint style — small towers, pointed windows and battlements — or in the rather sterner form of mock castles.

It is this coexistence of classical and romantic taste in architecture that makes the Regency period so fascinating. By studying the buildings of the first forty years of the nineteenth century we can appreciate the groundwork upon which the Victorian age created its architectural diversity.

Part Two
Building in Shropshire 1730-1840

The Large Country Houses

As we start looking more closely at the development of the built landscape in Shropshire during this period it is useful to deal first with the larger country houses, since they were usually in the forefront of fashion.

One fact that quickly becomes clear is that they were not built at a steady pace. After the flurry of provincial Baroque in the 1720s and 1730s there was a lull. Linley Hall (1742) introduced a version of Palladian style to the county, but it was not until about 1753 that the next major house, Delbury Hall, was built. The period 1760-80 saw seven new or remodelled houses, including Hatton Grange, Styche Hall, Walcot and Woodhouse. Most of the remainder date from the 1780s and after.

The reason for this lack of mid-eighteenth-century building is almost certainly an economic one. In the more fashionable counties the income of landowners could derive from a variety of sources such as mercantile activities, emoluments from major public offices or the proceeds of colonial administration, but wealth in Shropshire was heavily dependent on agricultural prosperity. Urban growth and industrial development during the late eighteenth century created ever-growing markets for farmers, and the French wars between 1793 and 1815 boosted the demand for food. Many farmers became rich and so did their landlords, so perhaps it is not surprising that so much major country building took place at the end of the century.

The architectural consequence was that the period of pure Palladianism before 1750 hardly touched Shropshire, and it took the later neo-classical movement to produce the county's best-known Palladian house, Attingham Park. Nevertheless it is possible to see a dramatic change of taste early in the eighteenth century, exemplified in Delbury Hall at Diddlebury in Corvedale. As we have seen, the fashion in the 1720s and 1730s was for showy embellishment, with giant pilasters, quoins, string courses and eaves pediments, but little more than twenty years later Delbury was built with an almost totally plain façade, the only concession to ornament being dentillated brickwork beneath the eaves. This change to severity and the restrained use of decoration is the most obvious characteristic of houses in town and country during the later eighteenth century.

Because so many of the large new (or remodelled) country houses of the period appeared quite late, they reflect the greater diversity of styles that were evident in the 1780s and after. The chaste neo-classical fashion, for example, is seen at its best at Attingham Park, and in a more modest form at Aston Hall, Oswestry. Both are of the 1780s. The Picturesque taste arrived tardily in Shropshire, but produced a number of new and modified houses, including Hawkstone's 'Citadel', Apley Park, Rowton Castle, Sibdon Castle,

Delbury Hall (c. 1753) illustrates the striking trend during the eighteenth century away from the fussy embellishments of provincial Baroque (see Cound Hall pictured in Part 1). It has no stone dressings and a minimum of decoration on the façade. Only the entrance door is emphasised.

Quatford Castle and Lilleshall Hall (neo-Tudor). Dating from 1790 to 1840, they indicate the persistent popularity of castellation.

The period of the Greek Revival covered roughly the same years and a number of Shropshire landowners were attracted by it. The results can be seen at Acton Burnell Hall, Brogyntyn, Longford Hall, Millichope, Willey Hall, Astley House, and Oakley Park. The style was safe and conservative, ensuring a house of reassuring solidity, but it was not to the taste of all; a few enterprising men opted for the highly-individual designs that are usually lumped together under the name 'Regency'. It is impossible to define it precisely, but we recognise it when we look at the ironwork embellishment of The Lyth at Ellesmere, the elegant bow-front entrance at Caynton Hall near Shifnal, the ultra-simple dignity of Decker Hill, the glassed arcade that is an integral part of the façade at Longner Hall, and the delightful Italian villa of Cronkhill (the last two being the work of John Nash).

This does not mean that the small number of major houses built in the mid-eighteenth century are uniform in appearance, but they have a basic sameness because their builders shared certain characteristics — a distaste for obvious embellishment, a pride in their brickwork and above all a comfortable sense of conforming to a fashion that was unlikely to pass quickly. Nor did it. The basic model of a three-, five- or seven-bay brick house with two-and-a-half storeys, a low roof, plain sash windows and a 'classical' porch with columns or pilasters became enshrined in the pattern books and guaranteed the survival of the style well into the nineteenth century. Variations on the theme can be seen at Caynton House (Edgmond), the Mansion House at Ford, Hatton Grange, Leighton Hall and Walcot, as well as in dozens of 'middle-rank' houses. Occasionally the style could be raised to distinction, as at Robert Mylne's Woodhouse near Oswestry.

Few large country mansions of the period were brand new. The majority were reconstructions, remodellings or enlargements of existing houses, and there were various methods of carrying out the modifications. An older building could simply be encased within a new shell, as at Rowton Castle, or a new block built to hide the older one, as at Attingham Park or Woodhouse.

Longford Hall, c. 1795. The liking at this time for the heavy Grecian style brought stone back into favour. The giant portico, reminiscent of the Parthenon, was an essential feature, although here it is a porte-cochere *designed to accommodate carriages.*

Caynton House, near Edgmond — a fine example of the restrained taste of the later eighteenth century.

A more straightforward method was to construct extensions at the side in the form of detached flanking pavilions, a device exemplified at Hawkstone Hall and Moreville Hall. Sometimes a house could be instantly transformed by a major new feature, in particular a giant portico, as happened at Acton Burnell and Brogyntyn. In fact Brogyntyn is an excellent example of the process of modernisation. Most of the present house dates from the 1730s, when it incorporated an older building, and it would have been in the usual fussy Baroque style of the time. By the early nineteenth century it was seriously outdated, so a drastic remodelling took place; the house was refaced in ashlar, the Baroque embellishments were removed and a giant portico added to provide an instant Greek Revival appearance

Other Country Buildings

Before the middle of the eighteenth century rural houses could be divided into four broad categories — the mansions of the biggest landowners, the manor houses of the squirearchy, the yeomens' farmhouses and the makeshift homes of the landless labourers. The mansions were almost invariably constructed of brick or stone, but many of the manor houses were timber-framed, as were the vast majority of farmhouses and hovels. By 1840 this pattern had changed considerably, and the reasons had much to do with farming prosperity.

The agricultural wealth of the sixteenth and seventeenth centuries had been based mainly on wool production, although farmers close to the growing towns had started to diversify into milk, meat and corn. The eighteenth century saw a continuing rise in the urban population, together with the emergence of a new market in the increasingly prosperous industrial settlements on and around the Shropshire coalfield. The demand for food rose even more sharply towards the end of the century when the wars against France reduced imports, and the result was a rapid expansion of mixed farming in all but the hill regions of the county. In the rush to meet the demand farmers brought into cultivation great acreages of land which had previously been waste, and there was much rearrangement of holdings to create more efficient farms.

Unlike the Midland counties, Shropshire was not dramatically affected by Parliamentary enclosure — official Acts took second place to informal agreements among landowners — but the consequence of the move towards larger holdings and greater efficiency was a reshaping of the landscape. There had always been isolated farmsteads in the hills, but in the lowland areas of the county the general pattern had been one of farms grouped in a village or hamlet, with the surrounding fields being cultivated from this nucleus. Most of the timber-framed dwellings that still remain in our villages would once have been the houses of yeoman farmers.

While holdings were generally small and the land was chiefly used for grazing this system worked well enough, but the trend towards large self-contained holdings, with intensive cultivation and methodical cattle-breeding, required farms to be at the centre of their fenced fields. Thus was created the farming landscape with which we are familiar today. These developments

The new brick farmhouse isolated in its fields became a familiar sight during the eighteenth century. This example is at Shotatton, near Ruyton-XI-Towns.

brought about social changes too. The major landowners had new incentives to improve the farming potential of their estates, and agriculture became more and more a matter of close partnership between the landowner and his tenant farmers, with the owner providing capital for new farmhouses and buildings. Some of the squirearchy, many of them the descendants of the earlier yeomen, farmed their land personally, but others had social ambitions and preferred to let their farms and enjoy the income from rents. The general prosperity gave the tenant farmer a new social status, enabling him to adopt a comfortable lifestyle, while for the labourers there was full employment.

We have seen that one result of all this was the building of new and fashionable country mansions, but in addition there emerged a range of housing to suit the new social ladder. A study of the Ordnance Survey maps of Shropshire will reveal a great many houses standing in small parks; they were the homes of the minor landowners, the squires of their districts and the backbone of local government in the eighteenth century. Their houses might well have been built in the seventeenth century or during the Queen Anne period, but many of them were able to finance new houses in the Georgian style, constructed by anonymous local builders from pattern books. They tend to have a certain sameness about them — built of brick, with three or five bays, and without much embellishment apart from a columned and pedimented porch. Whether they stand in gracious isolation, or have farm buildings close by depends on the degree of social ambition of the original owner.

Rather more obvious to the present-day traveller are the Georgian farmhouses, isolated in their fields. Typically they are of four-square appearance, of three bays and three storeys, presenting an uncluttered façade at the front but having functional outbuildings at the rear. Very often the formal front conceals an older timber-framed structure, remodelled and given extra height, but many were brand new, built fairly economically from pattern books by estate owners for their tenant farmers. They may look homely today, but to their first occupants they represented a new kind of fashionable living. In many cases their large brick barns survive nearby, an indication of the changing scale of farming.

This type of new brick farmhouse was largely confined to the lowland areas. In the hills stone was the preferred material, and there is no lack of examples. Many of them are timber-framed structures that received a casing of stone in the seventeenth century, but others are fairly palatial and reflect the fact that the agricultural prosperity of the eighteenth and early nineteenth centuries extended to sheep farmers too. There was a growing market for wool, both in the developing textile towns of the north of England and in Welsh towns like Newtown and Glyn Ceiriog.

And what of the farmworkers? Contemporary writers are unanimous in agreeing that for most of the eighteenth century farmworkers lived in appallingly cramped and squalid conditions. If they were single they usually had quarters on the farm; if they were married the best they could hope for was a tiny cottage or a subdivision of a redundant timber-framed farmhouse. The useful life of buildings like this was frequently prolonged by casing them in brick or stone. The housing would probably be in the local village, which meant that many workers had a lengthy walk to and from the farms. If this sort of accommodation was not available the labourers had to follow the example of their forefathers and build their own hovels wherever they could. Elsewhere in England there were a few experiments with 'model villages' for estate workers, but these were not to appear in Shropshire until well into the Victorian period.

Employees of the wealthier landowners might occasionally find themselves provided with new housing as a result of the fashion in the later eighteenth century for 'rustic' cottages in fanciful styles. Many architects produced pattern books to enable an employer to sprinkle picturesque buildings across his estate and so improve the view. The most obvious survivors of this fashion

As farmers moved out of the villages their former timber-framed houses were often converted into cottages for farm labourers. This house at Pontesbury was sub-divided into three tiny units.

are the roadside lodges, often the result of designs that border on the fantastic, but sometimes it is possible to see one of the popular 'Gothick' cottages with thatch and pointed windows. There is one (actually a semi-detached pair in disguise) next to the garage at Atcham. Occasionally this liking for the self-consciously Picturesque would extend to grander buildings such as the Citadel, a dower-house near Hawkstone Hall, or Cronkhill, which was designed by John Nash in Italianate style to house the Attingham Park agent.

It is not easy now to find authentic examples of eighteenth-century labourers' dwellings, thanks to the modern passion for 'restoring' timber-framed cottages, but there would appear to be a group opposite the village shop in Roden, on the B5062 east of Shrewsbury, and another close to the church gate in Pontesbury. There are also terraces of small timber-framed cottages in Acton Burnell and on the south-eastern outskirts of Craven Arms.

The country buildings described so far were often new and unusual, but at least they had a familiar rural purpose. The one distinctly new phenomenon of the later eighteenth century was the appearance of middle-class village houses. They are easily recognisable today as versions of Georgian or Regency town houses, standing beside the village street on fairly modest plots and perhaps screened from the road by a tall hedge.

Sometimes they were the homes of the local doctor or parish priest, but often their occupants were people with no traditional place in the countryside — ex-colonial administrators, former army and navy officers and retired professional men. After a century of metropolitan dominance in fashion there seems to have been a movement after 1800 back to 'wholesome' country living. Reduced incomes, of course, may also have been a factor.

Building in the Towns

The eighteenth century saw some radical changes in Shropshire's urban landscapes. Throughout the sixteenth and seventeenth centuries towns had been developing steadily, reflecting the general prosperity of the countryside and the ever-increasing complexity of rural economics. Farmers had always needed markets, but as they became wealthier they and their families demanded a range of additional services — tailors, shoemakers, dressmakers, haberdashers, grocers — befitting their new status. This growing demand for what had previously been luxuries resulted in a thriving carrier business, with the towns becoming distribution points for goods brought from London or major provincial cities. The continual improvements to the county's road system that made this possible also encouraged social and business travel for which the towns duly provided facilities.

By 1730 the larger towns had been transformed from huddled settlements within defensive walls to quite sophisticated areas of concentrated commercial activity. One consequence was a rising level of wealth among a wide range of entrepreneurs, from powerful merchants to small shopkeepers; another was the emergence of a prosperous middle-class of lawyers, doctors and other professional men. For much of the seventeenth century the time-honoured custom of 'living over the shop' persisted, but after 1700 there was a noticeable tendency for those who could afford it to move into new houses, and the first fashionable districts began to appear.

It would be misleading to call these developments 'suburbs' because they were often little more than new streets. Among the obvious examples are Belmont in Shrewsbury, Dodington in Whitchurch, Broad Street and Mill Street in Ludlow, Lower Brook Street in Oswestry, Shropshire Street in Market Drayton and East Castle Street in Bridgnorth. They are important because they established the idea of like living with like — a new awareness of social distinctions. Hitherto status had been marked by the size and design of individual houses rather than by residential area, but from the early eighteenth century onwards social 'zoning' was to become a powerful factor in the changing urban landscape.

The process was reinforced by the new concept of the town as a social centre. There had long been a tradition of mutual hospitality among the county's wealthier landowners, but organised entertainment was almost unknown if we discount traditional fairs and seasonal celebrations. It was the example of spa towns like Bath, Cheltenham and Leamington that led to the

A typical large urban residence of the later eighteenth century in Quarry Place, Shrewsbury. The characteristic features are the five bays, the two-and-a-half storeys, the enriched doorcase and the eaves parapet. The slightly-arched windows are unusual.

introduction in Shropshire of novel events like concerts, theatre parties, dances and race meetings, where social equals could meet and be seen in fashionable surroundings. By the late eighteenth century there were acknowledged 'seasons' in Ludlow and Shrewsbury, and many landowners took them seriously enough to build town houses as outposts of their estates. When the Marquess of Bath built what is now Swan Hill Court House in the 1760s he no doubt set the seal on the Quarry district of Shrewsbury as the most desirable area in which to live.

When the wealthier citizens moved into a smart new residential district the houses which they left behind would be occupied by people of more modest income climbing another step up the housing ladder. These people were fashion-conscious too, so the appearance of the old timber-framed buildings that formed the town centres began to change dramatically as people realised the possibilities of remodelling.

For comparatively little outlay it was possible to have the front of a timber house replaced by a façade that had all the desired features — brickwork, a regular pattern of rectangular sash windows, an eaves cornice and a porch embellished with columns and pediment. The general 'Georgian' character of so many Shropshire towns owes less to the building of new houses than to this process of 'casing', which could sometimes be very ambitious. For example, it was almost impossible to achieve the popular two-and-a-half-storey façade without raising the roof considerably, and it was often necessary to rearrange the room layout to fit the new window pattern. When this could not be completely achieved a 'blind' glazed window would often be installed to regularise the façade. Alternatively a window could be painted on to the brickwork, a device that is commonly (and often mistakenly) assumed to be the result of the window tax of the late eighteenth century.

Sometimes all the front timbers would be relocated to accommodate the brick façade, in which case the effect could be indistinguishable from a new building; more often the main structural timbers were retained, giving an uncertain shape to the window openings and a tell-tale 'sag' to the brickwork. Demolition and redevelopment from the Victorian period to the present day has frequently exposed the sides of these houses, revealing the original timber framing.

Every town centre in the county has its share of brick-cased timber framing, but it is particularly noticeable in the wide main street at Newport, while Ellesmere's St John's Hill is a striking example of a residential street given the treatment.

The style of urban architecture favoured throughout most of the eighteenth century was remarkably consistent. Idiosyncratic experiments in the Baroque style, exemplified by Hardwick House in Shrewsbury and Idsall House in Shifnal, gave way after 1730 to a generally severe character with little embellishment. Tall rectangular sash windows, often with keystones, established a regular façade, and in a double-fronted house the window over the doorway would often be 'enriched' with decoration to its surround. The two-and-a-half storey arrangement was universally popular, allowing for family rooms on two floors, servants' accommodation in the attics and the kitchens in a basement. Roofs were shallow-pitched and frequently concealed behind a

A rare example of Regency style in Dinham, Ludlow, with a hooded window and balcony, and an oriel window on the street side.

balustrade or cornice which might incorporate an eaves pediment. At street level the front door was the focal point, emphasised either by an elaborate surround including pilasters and pediment or by a projecting porch on columns.

The use of builders' pattern books allowed these features to be adapted for houses of many different sizes from large detached mansions to small terraced villas, and the style remained popular well into the Victorian period. So entrenched was it that we find only isolated examples in the county of urban 'Regency' architecture — the stuccoed terraces with balconies that are so familiar in spa towns.

A major innovation during this period was the widespread acceptance of the terrace and semi-detached house and we probably have to look to London and to the spa towns again for an explanation. Eighteenth-century London witnessed a number of prestigious residential developments sponsored by the great landowners, together with less ambitious schemes undertaken by individual builders. In both cases the object was to create as many houses as possible while retaining an air of distinction. Terraces were economical and space-saving, and Italian architects had long ago established the principle of the 'palace front', by which a terrace could be embellished on its façade to give the illusion of a single great house. This device, coupled with dignified layout (for example, around a pastoral square) proved sufficiently attractive for discerning clients who could not afford a very expensive detached house or who wanted a London house for occasional use.

The first terraces consisted of quite palatial houses, but once they had proved acceptable in aristocratic circles it was possible to scale them down in size to suit a wide range of buyers or tenants. The popularisation of the terrace was even easier in spa towns like Bath since they catered less for residents than for seasonal visitors, and there was little objection to a terraced house as a home for short-term renting provided that one's neighbours were the right sort of people. The influence of developments like the Royal Crescent at Bath was incalculable.

Little wonder then that a custom established in the most fashionable circles should be accepted among the middle-class residents of Shrewsbury or Ludlow. In fact Shropshire has no examples of ambitious planned terraces of the Georgian or Regency period, although it is possible to find developments of half-a-dozen houses or less. More common is the terrace created by a number of different builders working to a uniform height but using individual designs and making no attempt at unification. The results could be just as harmonious.

The semi-detached house had no aristocratic sanction, and it proved necessary to apply the principle of 'unification' here too, so that the two houses could be made to look like one. Common devices were a single eaves pediment or an elaborate porch accommodating both front doors, and it proved an attractive solution for middle-class clients. The same technique could result in gracious and unassuming lower-middle-class terraces like Whitehall Street in Shrewsbury and Porkington Terrace in Oswestry.

The early nineteenth century also saw the first appearance in towns of terraces of artisan housing — primitive perhaps, but a welcome improvement on small tenements over shops or overcrowded courts beyond the main streets. These early terraces, unlike their later Victorian counterparts, often had a kind of simple elegance that in our own day has ensured their conversion into bijou 'cottages', but it is occasionally possible to see quite authentic survivals; there is a short row in Whitburn Street, Bridgnorth, but perhaps the most striking example is Charlotte Row at Ellesmere.

Before the eighteenth century the concept of streetscape had been virtually non-existent. Indeed, one of the charms of small English towns is the haphazard, unplanned mixture of buildings along their principal streets. Shropshire towns never acquired large areas of formally laid-out streets and squares, but in the later part of the century developers were obviously becoming conscious of the total effect of houses in a street, giving them a general congruity of style and often a consistent height. Ludlow's Broad Street and Mill Street are famous, but St John's Hill and Quarry Place in Shrewsbury and East Castle Street in Bridgnorth are also fine examples.

Churches

It was noted in the previous volume that very few new churches were built in Shropshire during the period 1540-1730, and the mid-eighteenth century saw little change in the situation. Building was confined to a small number of villages like Kinnerley, Montford, Cardeston and Longdon-on-Tern, and was the result of individual philanthropy.

During the period 1780-1840, however, there was a sudden upsurge of interest in church building in both town and country. It was inspired partly by the Evangelical revival following Wesley's breach with the Church of England, bringing a new wave of religious enthusiasm to the established church after a long period of laxity. Another motive was a rather more secular feeling among prosperous middle-class people that their seemly new houses ought to be matched by seemly new places of worship; the ever-increasing refinement of society was not well served by leaky and dilapidated churches. A third factor may well have been the general interest in architecture among wealthy country landowners, who saw a parish church in the same light as a new entrance lodge or a new group of estate cottages — something to improve a picturesque view.

The formation of the Church Building Society in 1818 promoted an interest in the subject, while the Church Building Act soon afterwards provided funds administered by a Commission for the building of new churches where none existed, mainly in the new industrial towns and expanding city suburbs. St Luke's, Ironbridge, was a 'Commissioners' church'. Otherwise Shropshire did not qualify noticeably under this provision, but it helped to fuel the new enthusiasm which produced about thirty new churches in the county in addition to modifications of existing buildings.

The designs reflect a basic division of architectural opinion between the claims of 'classical' and 'Gothic'. It was inevitable that the trend towards Renaissance and classical building should include church design, and the innovators in this respect were Wren and his colleagues who had the task of rebuilding London churches after the Great Fire. Their wish to produce 'Basilica' churches that resembled Roman temples happened to suit the new Protestant ideas of worship. The medieval churches conformed in design to the Catholic precept that the Mass was a mystery not to be openly shared by the congregation, who came to 'hear' the service but not to participate fully.

The abandoned church at Longford (c. 1805) is castellated — no doubt at the whim of the landowner.

Thus the chancel was emphatically divided from the nave, usually by a screen. Post-Reformation worship encouraged full participation by a congregation who were entitled to see and hear everything, so the new churches were planned in an essentially theatrical way, with the chancel as a stage. The analogy was usually reinforced by the installation of a gallery.

Basically, the new classical churches were simple rectangles housing nave and chancel together, a design that appeared in Shropshire in a homely way when a new church was built at Minsterley in the 1680s. Minsterley, however, was something of a Baroque muddle and had little classical elegance. The pioneering classical church in the county was St Alkmund's, Whitchurch (1712), a building with all the hallmarks of the new style — Tuscan columns, decorated ceiling, pilasters in the sanctuary, fine woodwork, a gallery on three sides and the whole interior brightly lit by big windows with clear glass.

St Alkmund's was a happy accident — the previous church had collapsed and there was no alternative but to rebuild — and the prevailing ecclesiastical apathy of that time ensured that it remained a unique prototype in Shropshire for most of the eighteenth century. In the 1790s, however, the classical design was adopted for a series of important town churches. Thomas Telford used it for St Mary's, Bridgnorth, St Michael's, Madeley, and St Leonard's, Malinslee, while George Steuart was responsible for All Saints, Wellington and St Chad's, Shrewsbury, which is the supreme Shropshire example of sophisticated classical church architecture.

The style was, however, essentially urban, and remained a minority taste, except among Nonconformists, whose chapels reflected the amphitheatre style well into the twentieth century. Among Anglicans the brief flowering of the classical trend was supplanted by a feeling that churches ought to be Gothic — a sense that ecclesiastical style had been established in the Middle Ages and should not be lightly changed. It was perhaps inevitable that this feeling should prevail in a conservative rural county where the small medieval parish church was the norm, and it was reinforced by a taste for the Gothic style among many landowners at the turn of the eighteenth century.

Thus the vast majority of new Shropshire churches built between 1780 and 1840 were Gothic in design. The term 'Gothic' includes a variety of medieval styles — Early English, Decorated, Perpendicular — and all were explored in scholarly reproductions or adaptations that ranged from town churches in Shrewsbury, Oswestry and Wellington to village churches at Badger, Cressage, Cruckton, Shelve, Tilstock and Eaton Constantine. There were occasional departures from the Gothic pattern; St Catherine's at Whitchurch was built in a distinctive Grecian fashion, while there was a return to Norman style at Grinshill and Albrighton (Shrewsbury).

These new churches were not, of course, copies of medieval churches, since they had to be adapted for Protestant worship. Indeed, several architects succeeded in getting the best of both worlds by combining a Gothic exterior with the spacious, open, well-lit interior associated with the classical churches. St Luke's, Ironbridge and St Alkmund's, Shrewsbury are examples. Most village churches were a compromise of the kind which we now accept as normal — a nave and chancel separated by a broad chancel arch that suggested a division without obstructing the congregation's view of the altar.

The former Nonconformist chapel in Town Walls, Shrewsbury, was built in 1834 in elegant Greek style with tall, round-headed windows and prominent twin porches.

The pulpit and lectern were placed prominently in front of the congregation, and in most cases provision was made in the chancel for choir-stalls — a novel phenomenon in the early nineteenth century.

Nonconformist Chapels

A survey of the characteristic buildings of this period would not be complete without some mention of the Nonconformist chapels.

The Shropshire countryside, where most people depended for their livelihoods on conservative landowners, was never a very promising recruiting ground for dissenters, and it is noticeable that country chapels tend to be in isolated spots out of the public eye. But major towns like Shrewsbury, Ludlow, Oswestry and Bridgnorth seem to have had enthusiastic Presbyterian or Baptist congregations quite early in the eighteenth century. The no-man's-land of the Shropshire coalfield was a different matter. The established ironmasters had already introduced a strong Quaker tradition there, and small independent churches found a ready following. John Fletcher, Vicar of Madeley from 1760 to 1785 was a noted Evangelical who strongly supported the Methodist cause, and there was no conventional Anglican presence in Ironbridge until 1836, nor in Coalbrookdale until the 1850s. It is not surprising that after 1800 the Severn Gorge became an active centre of Nonconformist evangelism within the county.

The dissenting movement reached its first peak of popularity in the early

1830s, helped, no doubt, by the militancy of working-class movements at the time. Consequently a very large number of chapels date from this decade, and at the same time several existing eighteenth-century buildings were either demolished or replaced. Others were adapted, to the detriment of their original character. A similar process took place in the later nineteenth century at another peak of enthusiasm.

As a result, the county has comparatively few notable examples of pre-Victorian chapels, and certainly very few of architectural significance. Among the exceptions are the early Baptist chapel at Broseley (1742), the former Congregational church in Arthur Street, Oswestry (1830), the Congregational church at Newport (1832), the Wesleyan chapel at Madeley Wood (1837) and the Independent meeting place in Chapel Street, Wem (1775, altered 1834). They all to some extent show an awareness of contemporary style, but the most fashion-conscious building is probably the former Ebenezer Chapel in Town Walls, Shrewsbury, an uncompromisingly classical structure of 1834.

These are all urban buildings, but dotted around the Shropshire countryside are smaller and homelier chapels of the same period. They are usually unpretentious, the only concession to their function being the design of their windows, which are either vaguely Gothic or round-headed in the classical manner. Good examples are to be found at Wilcott, near Nesscliffe (1834), Ruyton-XI-Towns (1833), and Harmer Hill (1833).

Public Buildings

A survey of public buildings erected in Shropshire during the eighteenth and

Lacon Child's School, Cleobury Mortimer, dates from c. 1740 and has the hipped roof with dormers that was fashionable thirty years earlier.

early nineteenth centuries reveals an impressive range of new social concerns. It is significant that the entrance to Shrewsbury prison, completed in 1793, carries a bust of John Howard, the prison reformer, and the building was obviously the result of philanthropic intentions. The same motives inspired the founders of what was to become the Royal Salop Infirmary, built in Shrewsbury in 1830 and a pioneering achievement in national terms. Hosyer's Almshouses at Ludlow were rebuilt in the 1750s, new almshouses appeared at Bridgnorth in 1792, and Captain Coram's Foundling Hospital was established in Shrewsbury in 1765, but a new and rather grimmer approach to the problem of poverty is indicated by purpose-built workhouses at Oswestry (1792) and Shifnal (1817).

The explosion in educational provision was to come later in the nineteenth century, but it is worth noting that Oswestry Grammar School moved to new premises in 1776 and that there was a major rebuilding of Adams Grammar School, Newport, in the 1820s. Ironbridge was provided with a new infants' school in 1834 and Cleobury Mortimer had its own school by 1740.

The Buttermarket at Ludlow, built in 1744, was the first in a succession of similar buildings. A market house formed part of the nucleus of the new town of Ironbridge in the 1790s, and market halls appeared in the early nineteenth century in Church Stretton, Wem, Whitchurch and Market Drayton. The latter was simply a covered space, but the rest followed the pattern set more than two hundred years earlier at Shrewsbury — an open-arched ground floor with rooms above that could be used for civic purposes. Ellesmere acquired its distinctive town hall in 1833, while at about the same time a new Shire Hall, designed by the celebrated Robert Smirke in the 1830s, was sited in the Square at Shrewsbury. It has since been demolished. One new feature of late eighteenth-century life was the taste for public entertainment, mainly in the form of concerts and dances. Shrewsbury and Ludlow both had fashionable 'seasons', and for a long time the wealthier citizens gathered socially in *ad hoc* accommodation — The Lion Inn at Shrewsbury, for example, had an elegant assembly room. It was not until well into the nineteenth century that the first purpose-built premises for public entertainment appeared, and Shrewsbury's Music Hall (1840) was a considerable innovation. In the same year assembly rooms were combined with a new courthouse at Ludlow.

The Classical Orders

The use of the classical Orders was an integral part of so much architecture of the period that it is essential to have a grasp of the terminology. A feature such as a porch or a portico, if classically correct, was composed of various elements. A column had a base, a shaft and a capital, and it supported an 'entablature' composed of an architrave, a frieze and a pediment. These elements are shown in simplified form in the accompanying diagram.

The detailed design of the structure had to conform to one of the Orders, the choice of which depended originally on the function of the building — for example, the Corinthian Order was reserved for recreational buildings. (This rule was often ignored in English architecture.)

St John's Hill, Shrewsbury — an example of conscious streetscaping. The houses are individually designed and probably more than one builder was involved, but they are of uniform height and general character.

Cound Hall illustrates the provincial Baroque style in favour between 1700 and 1730. Each façade is heavily articulated with giant pilasters, string courses and eaves cornices.

Cronkhill — a light-hearted Italianate villa of about 1800 in the characteristic style of John Nash, exemplifying the more relaxed style of the Regency period.

A startling array of mock-medieval features at Quatford Castle (1830).

A five-bay house in Broad Street, Ludlow. The enrichment of the central first-floor window was a popular feature, but here the attic window has received the same treatment. The ground floor windows are in early nineteenth-century style and are probably replacements.

An innovatory terrace development of five houses in Town Walls, Shrewsbury. Erected in about 1840, they have a grooved stucco ground floor, recessed porches and exceptionally large first-floor windows.

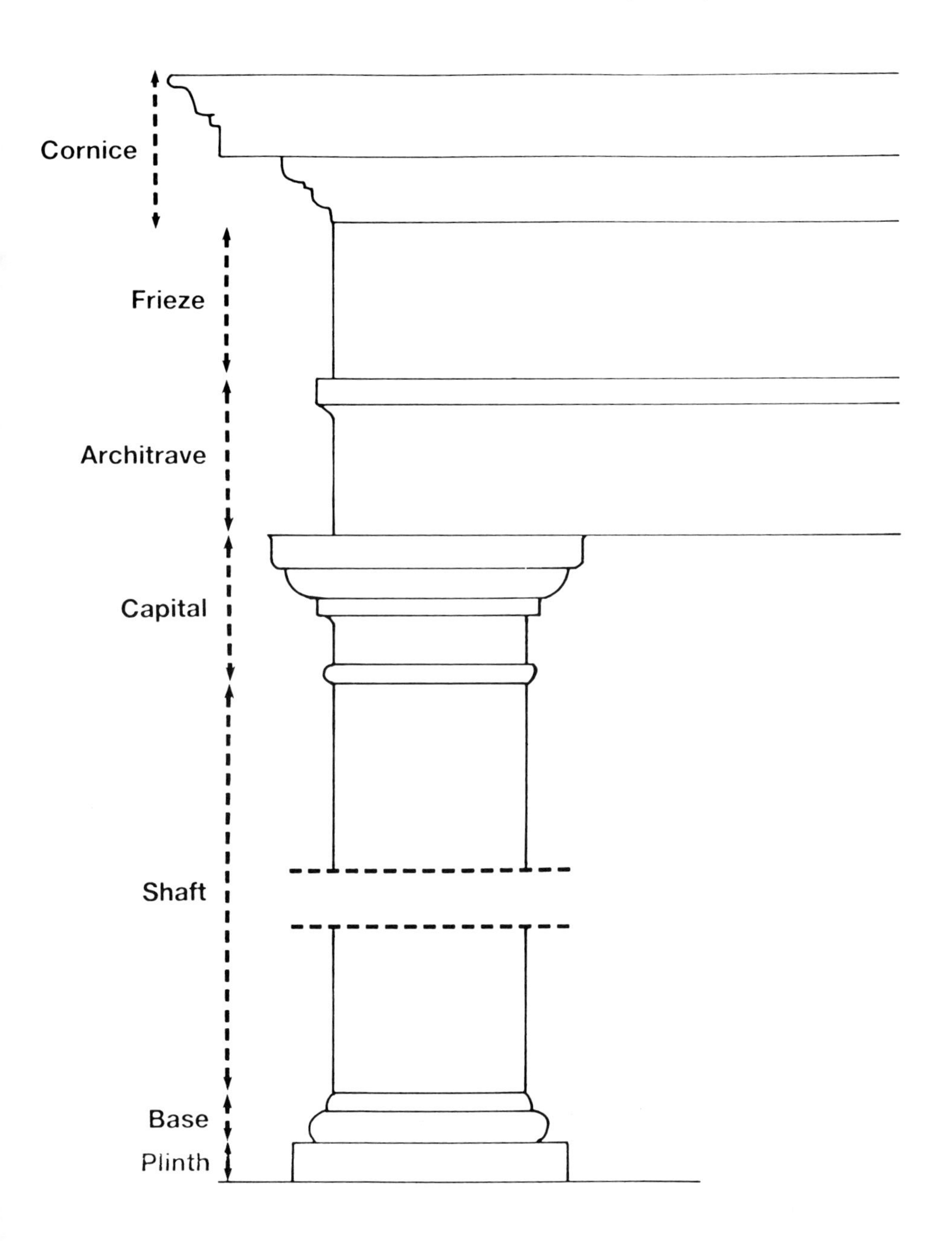

The parts of a classical columnal structure

Technically there were six Orders, but in practice we are concerned with four — Doric, Tuscan, Ionic and Corinthian. They are most readily identified by looking at the top, or capital, of the column, and the different designs are as follows:

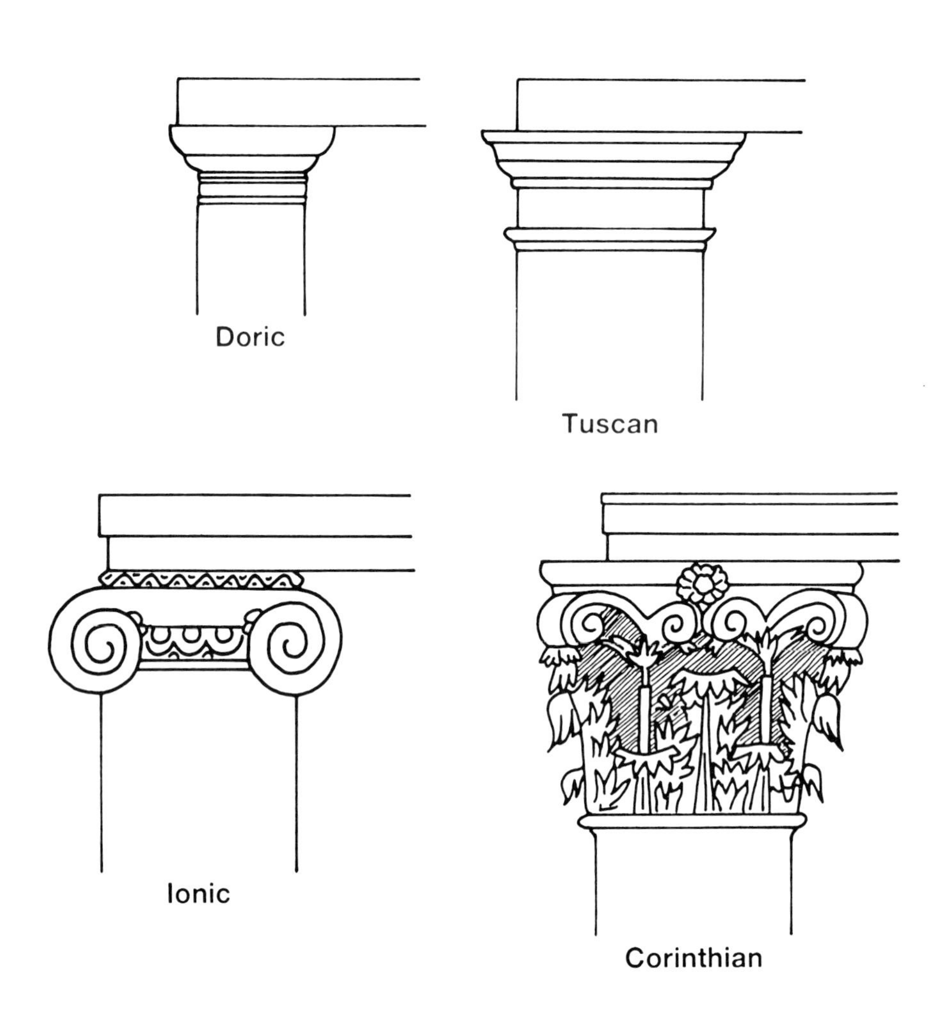

The principal Classical Orders

The Orders were also applied to pilasters used on the façade of a house.

Part Three
Industry and Transport

Introduction

During the period 1730-1840 Shropshire's industrial revolution reached its peak and faded. It was based on the pioneering achievements of a few energetic entrepreneurs, and once their lessons had been learnt it was inevitable that heavy industry should move to areas with much greater natural resources. We shall be concerned here with that brief period when the Severn Gorge led the world in the production and use of iron; the industries which flourished in the nineteenth century — particularly ceramics, lead-mining and quarrying — will be discussed in the volume on the Victorian period.

There is a popular misconception that Shropshire's industrial history began with the arrival at Coalbrookdale of Abraham Darby I. This was certainly an important event, but the cautious Darby was hardly a man to stick a pin in a map when deciding to relocate his Bristol ironworks. If Shropshire can claim to have been the birthplace of the Industrial Revolution, the basic reason lies in the natural resources of the area surrounding the Severn Gorge, and these had been tapped for a variety of purposes for 200 years before Darby's development of a coke-burning furnace for iron production.

Before the middle of the eighteenth century the attraction of the area for

The Iron Bridge.

small-scale industrialists had been not only the presence of coal, iron and limestone, but also the abundance of timber for producing charcoal, then an essential fuel for the furnaces. The production of charcoal was no longer a matter of indiscriminately felling trees over an ever-wider area; the system of coppicing allowed the replacement of timber and had become an important commercial business in its own right.

Nevertheless, the limited supply of charcoal and the slow production process was the biggest single restraint on iron production, and it was Darby's success with coke-burning furnaces during the early years of the eighteenth century that led to the remarkable expansion and industrial pre-eminence of the Severn Gorge until the end of the century.

There is little point in attempting yet another background history of the period since the story has been told in a number of readily-accessible books and pamphlets. What we are concerned with here is the industrial legacy of the Gorge and what remains to be seen today, and we are fortunate that there *is* so much to see. Whatever reservations we may have about the museum approach to industrial history, we have to acknowledge the tremendous achievement of the Ironbridge Gorge Museum Trust in preserving much that might otherwise have disappeared with the development of the new town of Telford.

Gazetteer of Sites and Buildings

(Map references are to OS sheet 127.)

Coalbrookdale

Rosehill House in Darby Road (665050). A fashionable residence of the mid-eighteenth century much smartened up by restoration. Its original brick façade showed a style that combined modern taste (plain windows with flat brick arches) and older fashion (prominent stone quoins). The fine entrance has an arched doorcase and pediment supported by console brackets.

(The next house down the hill, altered over the years, was undergoing drastic renovation at the time of writing, and its final form remains to be seen.)

No. 48 Darby Road has a six-bay asymmetrical front, drip mouldings to the windows and columned and pilastered porch.

Teakettle Row is perched above the large houses. It is an interesting terrace of very early workers' cottages (c. 1740). There are six units, not planned as an entity but given a roughly uniform exterior which features segment-headed windows and dormers set into the eaves.

The **'Great Warehouse'** of 1843 is a fortress-like building with iron-framed windows, topped by an incongruously flamboyant cupola added later. In its yard is the **Old Darby Furnace** under a protective cover. It is an industrial monument of immense importance — enlarged over the years, it was the furnace used for Abraham Darby I's new coke-smelting process in the early eighteenth century. Behind it is the face of the dam retaining the **upper furnace pool**, which supplied the early motive power to the bellows. The pool, once an ornamental lake, is now stagnant.

Carpenter's Row, Coalbrookdale — a terrace of eighteenth-century workers' cottages.

A former **boys' school and corn mill** stand beyond the 'village green' (669049). The school, now two houses, has iron-framed windows with small panes, round-headed on the first floor and embellished with drip mouldings on the ground floor. Behind it the former three-storey mill has similar features. They are probably both of the early nineteenth century.

Engine Row, opposite the old school (670049), was built in the 1780s as workers' housing but has now been modernised and renovated to the point of losing its character.

Carpenter's Row, at the head of the road down the valley (668047) is of the same period but has received little modernisation at the front. There are eight cottages, symmetrically planned; the extra doors at each end led to communal brewhouses.

Charity Row. The third surviving cottage terrace is in the road leading to the church (670045). These six houses have again been subjected to indiscriminate modernisation.

Ironbridge

The Severn Warehouse, on the outskirts of Ironbridge (668035) is an unusual Gothick structure of polychrome brick, dating from the 1840s but inspired by a fashion of twenty years earlier. Its pointed-arch windows and castellated turrets and chimneys give it an ecclesiastical air, reinforced by the apse at the western end.

The **Iron Bridge** (673035) was completed in 1779, providing a much needed road link between the industrial sites on each side of the Gorge. A consortium of local industrialists provided the finance and Thomas Farnolls Pritchard was originally retained as designer, the main requirement being a single arch that would not impede the heavy river traffic. Knowing that the Coalbrookdale

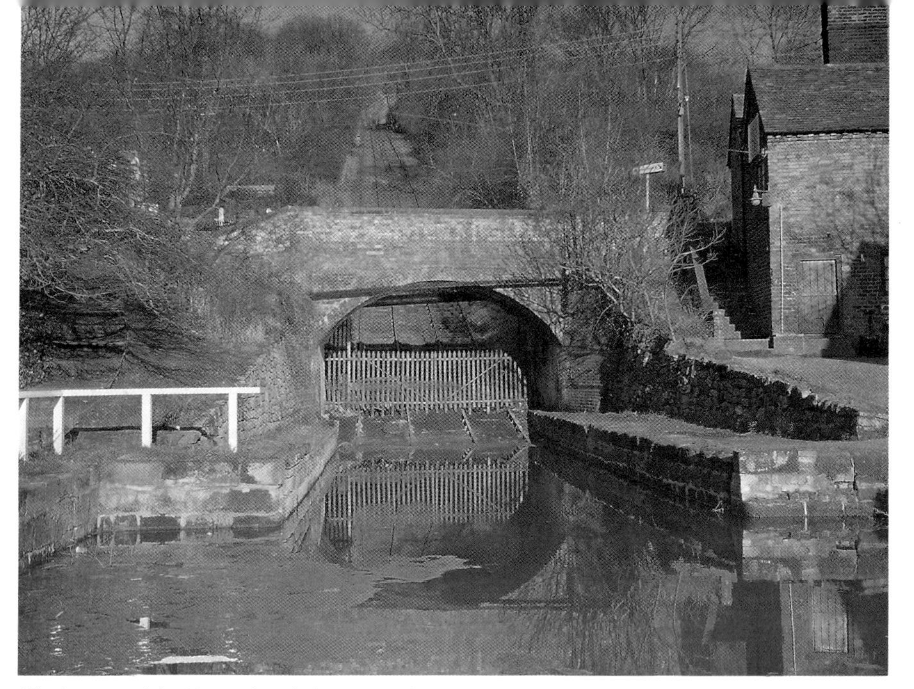

The bottom of the Hay inclined plane at Coalport. The rails on which the boats travelled can be seen descending through the trees from Blists Hill and passing beneath the road bridge to the lower canal basin.

works was capable of producing very large castings, Pritchard proposed a low structure combining iron and masonry, but after his death in 1777 Abraham Darby III amended the plans to provide for the much higher semi-circular arch we see today. It was to be the world's first iron bridge. Over 300 tons of ironwork was cast at the Darby furnace, and massive stone abutments were constructed on each side (the one on the town side remains, but the southern abutment had to be replaced in 1800 by a lighter arrangement). It was opened to public toll-paying traffic in 1781.

The Tontine Hotel and the Market Building face the bridge, and were planned as the nucleus of the new town of Ironbridge. The hotel has a plain five-bay frontage of two-and-a-half storeys, built in 1785 to a design by J. H. Haycock. It was hardly ambitious, but when an extension was added to the east side in the following year a more stylish effect was achieved. An enriched ground-floor window has a Venetian window above it, and there is a bulls-eye window in the eaves pediment.

The **Market Building**, close to the hotel, dates from about 1790 and is an unusual structure of five bays. The centre bay, pedimented and projecting slightly, contains a tall recessed arch accommodating the first- and second-floor windows. On the first floor there is a sequence of three tripartite windows with smaller ones between. The arches of the original open ground floor now contain shops.

St Luke's Church was a result of the Church Building Act of 1818, described in Part One. It stands above the hotel, and can be reached by a remarkable flight of steps that pass beneath the churchyard. Built between 1835 and 1837, it is a good example of a compromise between prevailing styles — the Gothic exterior houses a rectangular nave and chancel of the kind created by Telford and Steuart in their classical churches. The three-sided gallery is supported on cast-iron columns.

The Wesleyan Chapel on the Madeley Road (678035) is a fine example of its kind. Dating from 1837, it presents an imposing façade to the road, with its centre bay projecting and continuing up through the pediment, which is in fact the gable end. As at Madeley church, the gallery windows are round-headed and set above small rectangular windows on the ground floor. There is a dignified Grecian doorway.

The **Bedlam Furnace** stands beside the B4373 (677034), and is open to inspection. It was an extensive installation, and its fiery glow features in several lurid paintings of the Gorge.

Blists Hill (696035) is the largest of the museum sites and contains an extensive display of artefacts, machinery and buildings, including a reconstructed turnpike tollhouse and a squatter's cottage. A section of the Shropshire canal has been restored at its approach to the **Hay inclined plane**, described in the section on canals.

The **Tar Tunnel** can be seen at the foot of the Hay inclined plane (694025). It was excavated on the orders of William Reynolds, possibly as a means of mine drainage, and proved to be a profitable source of bitumen.

Shropshire's Canals

The story of canal development in the county begins in 1764 on the Shropshire coalfield, when Lord Gower planned a small canal to carry coal from his mines at Donnington Wood to Pave Lane, a point on the Wolverhampton road about two miles south of Newport. It was completed in 1768, and like the later canals on the Shropshire coalfield was designed for small 'tub boats', about 20 feet by 6 feet. Subsequently a short branch was constructed, leaving the main canal at Hugh's Bridge, just east of Lilleshall Abbey, and running due north to the village of Lilleshall. (This section is still marked on the modern Ordnance Survey map.) A third branch was cut from Willmore bridge, east of Lilleshall, up to Pitchcroft, where there were limeworks.

The level of the branch at Hugh's bridge was well below that of the main canal, and the original arrangement was for a crane system to transfer loads from one to the other. In the 1790s, however, this was replaced by an inclined plane which was originally used to transfer cargoes, although it appears that in later years the plane was altered to take the boats themselves.

This pioneering enterprise was followed in 1788 by a short canal built by the ironmaster William Reynolds to carry coal and iron ore from new mines at Wombridge to furnaces at Donnington Wood. It linked with the Donnington Wood Canal at a junction at Wrockwardine Wood.

In the same year Reynolds was also involved with a scheme to cut a canal from mines at Oakengates to his Ketley ironworks. A drop at the Ketley end led to the building of an inclined plane which is believed to have been the first in Britain to carry boats.

These three projects were all 'internal' canals with no links to the outside world, and it was inevitable that sooner or later there would be a demand for a canal link with the river Severn to supplement or replace the existing horse tramways. It was William Reynolds again who was principally involved in the plans for the Shropshire Canal, designed to run from the concentration of ironworks in the Ketley—Oakengates—Donnington Wood area due south to the river. Hitherto the only practicable transport route for heavy loads had been by horse tramway across to Coalbrookdale and down the valley.

The problem, of course, was the rise and fall of the ground and particularly the steep slope down to the river, but the successful opening of the inclined plane on the Ketley Canal had provided a blueprint for a new solution, and the Shropshire Canal was to have no fewer than three inclined planes.

Since this was a big and expensive undertaking, it was financed by a group of leading local industrialists. They included owners of works at Coalbrookdale, and so the final plan provided for a branch to serve that area. Linked to the western end of the Donnington Wood Canal, the new waterway was immediately raised 120 feet by means of an inclined plane at Wrockwardine Wood. Running due south, it passed through a tunnel at Snedshill, linked with the Ketley Canal and traversed another tunnel at Old Park. At Southall Bank the Coalport arm branched off (it actually terminated at Brierley Hill) while the main channel continued to a second inclined plane at Windmill Bank, where the level was lowered 126 feet. The final stretch passed across Blists Hill to the Hay, where a third incline lowered boats over 200 feet to a short stretch of canal running parallel to the Severn. From here the tub boats were hauled to a wharf where their cargoes could be transferred to river craft.

The revolutionary inclined planes avoided multiple locks, a great benefit in an area where water supply was not easy. Unfortunately only the Hay plane has survived in restorable form. It worked by floating the boats on to cradles which then traversed the incline on rails, their speed being controlled by a brake wheel. Empty boats could be hauled up by the weight of the full ones without the need for motive power. At the other end the cradles would be submerged, floating the boats off.

Having completed this link with the Severn in 1793, Reynolds was later to develop the riverside site as the new community of Coalport.

It was inevitable that this local canal activity should inspire more ambitious ideas, and in 1792 a consortium of mine-owners and Shrewsbury investors obtained Parliamentary approval for the Shrewsbury Canal. It was intended mainly as a means of transporting coal from the mines to the county town. Work started on the Shrewsbury Canal in 1793, and two years later Thomas Telford became involved when the original engineer died. The project was completed early in 1797.

Its course can still be traced, sometimes sketchily, on the Ordnance Survey map. To create the eastern link at Donnington Wood the company bought a mile of Reynolds' Wombridge Canal and built a new junction at Trench, where an inclined plane was installed. The channel then passed north of Wappenshall to Eyton, a stretch notable for its eleven locks, which had unusual lifting gates.

The route continued through Sleapford and Longdon-on-Tern, where Telford is credited with what is now regarded as the prototype for his great Pontcysyllte aqueduct. The original masonry aqueduct was washed away by floods in 1795, and the idea of replacing it with a cast-iron trough may or may not have been Telford's, but he certainly drew up the design, including a cantilevered towpath that was to be repeated at Pontcysyllte.

After Longdon, the canal turned south-west to pass Rodington and Withington, took a ninety-degree turn at Berwick, just north of Attingham Park, and entered the 970-yard Berwick Tunnel, which was unusual at the time in being equipped with a towpath. The final stretch was round the big loop of the Severn north-west of Shrewsbury and into a terminus at Howard Street.

Although this was the most elaborate canal project yet attempted in Shropshire it still did not provide an outlet to the national system; in fact it was designed for nothing larger than the small tub boats of the coalfield waterways. In 1835 the opportunity arose of linking the Shrewsbury Canal to the Birmingham and Liverpool line, and a channel was cut from a junction at Wappenshall through Newport to Norbury. However, the prospect of connecting Shrewsbury to the national waterway system was never realised. A few adaptations to allow the passage of full-sized narrow boats were started, but the scheme was abandoned.

The final canal development in Shropshire had a grandiose aim — nothing less than an attempt to link the Severn, Dee and Mersey with a system of waterways that would have their central junction at Welsh Frankton, near Ellesmere. The prime motive of the Ellesmere Canal Company was the fact that the extensive industrial workings in the Wrexham—Ruabon area had no easy outlets for their products; the proposed canal would provide access both to Liverpool in the north and to Bristol by way of the Severn.

There would be subsidiary benefits too. In the late 1790s the wars with France had increased the demand for home-produced food, and farmers were improving neglected land at a furious rate. One of the main requirements was lime, and the limestone quarries at Llanymynech had already shown potential for great profits. A proposal for a waterway to bring out the lime from Llanymynech and assist in its distribution throughout the county received immediate priority.

Telford's cast-iron aqueduct on the Shrewsbury Canal at Longdon-on-Tern.

After the initial meeting of promoters in 1791, two years were spent on engineering surveys. The original engineer had been the almost unknown John Duncombe from Oswestry, and his proposed route was governed by the engineering difficulties of a direct channel from Ellesmere to Chester, difficulties which included the rise and fall of the area north of Ruabon and crossings of the rivers Ceiriog and Dee. He proposed instead a circuitous route which would first link the Mersey with Chester, then use the existing Chester Canal to a point near Nantwich, then turn south-west to pass through Whitchurch and Overton to the Wrexham industrial area. Branches would run to Llanymynech and Shrewsbury.

Two years later, Duncombe had been replaced by the vastly-experienced William Jessop, assisted by Thomas Telford, who was allowed to take this part-time post while retaining his position as County Surveyor for Shropshire. Jessop returned to the discarded idea of a direct route south from Chester to the proposed junction at Welsh Frankton, confident that all the engineering problems could be overcome. His ideas were accepted.

The formal proposals were announced in 1793, and such was the power of 'canal mania' that, amid hectic scenes, almost a million pounds was immediately promised by subscribers. But the engineering realities soon began to loom large, and the initial euphoria was replaced by a period of uncertainty as the problems were tackled.

The subsequent story of the Ellesmere canal system, full of political and engineering controversies, is of specialist interest and has been told fully in books by Charles Hadfield and others. Briefly the stages of construction were as follows:

1. The cutting of a channel from Ellesmere Port across the Wirral to Chester, which made possible a link with the Chester Canal in 1797.

2. The completion in 1796 of the Llanymynech branch, starting at Welsh Frankton and ending at Carreghofa, just beyond Llanymynech. It was the first section to be operational.

3. The starting of work on the Shrewsbury section, which branched from the Llanymynech arm a short distance south of Welsh Frankton. The work proceeded until the channel had reached a point near Weston Lullingfields and was then abandoned at the point now called Weston-wharf. The original purposes had been to carry coal from the Wrexham coalfield to Shrewsbury and also lime from Llanymynech, but it was discovered that the Shrewsbury Canal from Donnington Wood was providing both services quite adequately. (The short arm nevertheless survived until 1917.)

4. The building of two miles of canal north of Ruabon in 1796, as a start to the vitally important link between the Wrexham industrial area and outlets on the Dee and Mersey. A formidable lock system was planned for the difficult terrain involved.

5. The bridging of the Dee at Froncysyllte — an enormous technical challenge. The ultimate answer is attributed to Telford, although it is not clear to what extent Jessop was involved. The recurring difficulty

with all aqueducts was the sheer bulk and weight of masonry and puddled clay, but Telford had already built a light structure in cast iron for the Shrewsbury Canal at Longdon-on-Tern, and this must have influenced the decision in 1795 to support a light iron trough on slender masonry arches, crossing the river at 120 feet without lowering the canal level. The result was the Pontcysyllte Aqueduct, the greatest marvel of the canal age.

6. The completion of the channel from Welsh Frankton to Froncysyllte, a length which included another major aqueduct at Chirk. This turned out to be a hybrid — an iron base embedded in substantial masonry — which may indicate some caution about the more revolutionary scheme nearby.
7. The start, in 1797, on a link between Welsh Frankton and the Chester Canal. This had been originally proposed as the main line to the Mersey, but had been discarded in favour of the more direct link from Ruabon. The Ellesmere Company undertook it reluctantly because the Chester Canal Company decided to enforce an almost-forgotten agreement made several years earlier. Progress proved laboriously slow. The terrain was difficult, particularly across Whixall Moss, and the tunnel at Ellesmere presented unexpected problems. The work included a short branch into Ellesmere, which then became the Company's headquarters, and an arm towards Prees which was never completed. In a final burst of activity the line was finished in 1805, connecting with the Chester Canal at Hurleston Junction near Nantwich.
8. The abandonment of work north of Ruabon on the grounds that it would not be economic.
9. The construction of a navigable channel between Pontcysyllte and Llangollen to carry a water supply from the Dee to the whole canal system.

This Llangollen arm was the final stage in an astonishing engineering feat which left its mark very firmly on the Shropshire countryside. The system did not work out as planned. There was no short link between Ruabon and the Dee and Mersey, nor was there an outlet to the Severn, so the ambitious plans to export coal, iron and limestone to the nation were never realised. But the seventy-mile network brought a reasonable financial return, distributing raw materials and general merchandise throughout the county.

Canal Gazetteer

The tub boat canals

The remains of the early tub boat canals of the Shropshire coalfield have been largely obliterated by the development of Telford, but a stretch of the Shropshire Canal has been preserved at the Blists Hill Museum, including the Hay inclined plane.

It is possible to walk beside a silted-up length of the Donnington Wood—Pave Lane waterway to the west of Lilleshall (127: 735164 to 127: 740152). Another length is visible at Lilleshall Abbey (127: 737140).

The Shrewsbury Canal

Very few substantial features survive.

In Hadley Park, Telford (127: 674130) one of the 'guillotine' locks, unique to the Shrewsbury Canal, has been preserved.

The **Longdon-on-Tern aqueduct**, constructed in cast iron to Telford's design, stands at 127: 617156.

The **Howard Street Warehouse** at the Shrewsbury Terminal is described in Part Five at the beginning of the section on Shrewsbury.

The Llanymynech arm of the Ellesmere Canal

This length was abandoned in 1936. Some restoration has taken place, but the canal is not open to navigation, and in places is completely dry. The whole length of the towpath can be walked. All references are to OS sheet 126.

371318: **Welsh Frankton junction**. This was the 'crossroads' of the Ellesmere Canal Company's ambitious scheme. The four locks forming the junction of the Llanymynech and Llangollen arms of the canal have been restored. Looking down the disused stretch, the building set back on the right was the canal tavern, while on the left are the lock-keeper's cottage and the boatbuilder's workshop. The toll office stands at the head of the locks.

369311: the beginning of the abandoned **Shrewsbury arm**.

360298: the **aqueduct** over the river Perry.

352277: **Rednal**. There is a 'roving bridge', where the towpath continues on

The top lock of the flight at Welsh Frankton before restoration. This was the starting point of the Llanymynech arm of the Ellesmere Canal.

the other side of the canal. The bridge was designed to allow horses to pass across without the need to disconnect the towrope.

340268: **Queens Head**. Within the canalside shed there is a tunnel for a tramway which brought sand from nearby pits for loading onto boats.

314250: **Maesbury Marsh**. An early canal settlement, where the wharf and its crane have been restored. The Navigation Inn is still in business. On each side of the canal are former workers' cottages, and a short distance to the north of the wharf is a large bow-fronted house of the kind built by the Company for senior officials.

304246: **Gronwyn bridge and wharf**. In the early nineteenth century this was the terminus of a tramway from coalpits south of Oswestry.

293235: **Crickheath wharf**. The wharf, on the west bank, is overgrown. A tramway ran to this point, bringing limestone from the quarries at Pant. A maintenance-man's cottage on the east bank has been restored.

277224: **Pant wharf**. The loading point for limestone from the quarries above the village. The bridge has an extra hole to allow the trucks to run through.

274218: **Rhiwl Refail**. A bank of limekilns stand close to the bridge. An incline rises behind them and at its top, beside the shop on the main road above, is a restored winding drum.

266210: **Llanymynech**. The main loading point and processing plant for limestone. A short distance east of the bridge the entrances to two wharves can be seen. At the time of writing there is a plan to make the whole site accessible to the public.

254203: **Carreghofa locks**. The point where the Llanymynech arm joined the eastern arm of the Montgomeryshire Canal. The locks have been restored, and there is also a lock-keeper's cottage at the lower lock, a tollhouse at the upper lock and the toll-officer's house between them.

The north-western (Llangollen) arm of the Ellesmere Canal

This is restored and open to navigation. The only industrial monument of any importance in Shropshire is the **Chirk Aqueduct** (126: 286373), after which the canal enters Wales. The aqueduct was a considerable engineering achievement, consisting of an iron trough embedded in masonry and carried on tall arches over the river Ceiriog. It is possible to walk the towpath by gaining access at Chirk Bank (126: 292372). A railway viaduct of c. 1848 runs parallel to the aqueduct.

The north-eastern arm of the Ellesmere Canal

At **Ellesmere** the short arm into the wharf (126: 398346) is still heavily used by boats. There is a wharf crane and a warehouse at the town end, and the bow-fronted Beech House, the former headquarters of the canal company, stands where the arm emerges into the main channel (126: 401343).

The **Ellesmere Tunnel** can be walked through at 126: 413340.

The **Prees arm** leaves the main canal at 126: 489354. There are counter-weighted lifting bridges at 126: 491349 and 126: 492346.

Part Four
Building Techniques 1730-1840

The eighteenth century saw the virtual disappearance of timber-framing as a primary building technique, although its characteristic appearance has been sentimentally revived at regular intervals. Brick became the favourite construction material, and at times it threatened to extinguish the great tradition of English stonemasonry, which was revived near the turn of the century only by the taste for imposing buildings in the Greek Revival style, a fashion sustained with enthusiasm and eccentricity by the Victorians.

Brickwork and Bricklayers

In the previous volume we saw that bricks were introduced into Shropshire before the middle of the sixteenth century. Although their value was quickly appreciated in the construction of safer chimneys, many decades elapsed before they were widely accepted as a primary building material.

The reasons are understandable. Building a large brick structure involved making the bricks on the spot, since it was out of the question to transport frequent heavy loads on the roads of the time, and not every site had the right clays. The skill of bricklaying had to be acquired by the masons who were willing to try it, and until well into the seventeenth century they seem to have been cautious about its structural strength compared to that of familiar stone. There was a feeling also that brick was not a suitable material for a gentleman's house, and it was not until the end of the seventeenth century that the material which had been fashionable for nearly a hundred years in the south-east finally became acceptable in Shropshire.

The new enthusiasm for brick owed much to Francis Smith of Warwick,

Artisans' cottages in Bridgnorth, built at the turn of the eighteenth century.

one of the most influential builders in the Midlands, who was active in Shropshire between 1700 and 1730. He and his imitators popularised the provincial Baroque style that is characteristic of so many town and country houses built in Shropshire during the first thirty years of the eighteenth century — a basic brick structure embellished with stone dressings in the form of quoins, pilasters, cornices and so on.

The vast increase in the number of brick dwellings of all kinds, together with the elevation of bricklaying into an art, was perhaps the most important single development in building during the Georgian period. The trend away from Baroque showiness towards greater restraint produced a desire for less fussy façades, and brick proved to be the ideal material. Its great appeal was its flexibility; it could provide perfectly plain surfaces but was also capable of being cut or carved to give almost any form of decorative feature.

The attractiveness of Georgian brick owes much to its colouring. The process of hand-manufacture in the small brickworks that sprang up all over Shropshire during the eighteenth century had unpredictable results. The rough and ready combination of ingredients and the unscientific burning could produce a range of reds and browns that blended in a mellow way, and the dark over-burnt bricks could be used to pattern a wall effectively. The rough texture also contributes to what we now regard as a pleasing contrast to modern machine-made bricks. Whether the original clients took the same view is another matter.

The techniques of the first bricklayers reflected not only their masons' training, but their suspicions about the bonding powers of bricks. Until the middle of the seventeenth century they tended to use 'English Bond', which certainly resulted in a secure wall, but used an excessive number of bricks.

A brick used with its long side showing is known as a 'stretcher', while one with its end showing is a 'header'. English Bond involved building a double 'skin' of bricks with no cavity between, with one course of bricks laid along the wall and the next course laid across it to tie the skins together — in other words alternate courses of headers and stretchers. As confidence grew, more economical techniques emerged, such as a course of headers for every three or four courses of stretchers. By the eighteenth century the generally-accepted technique for good-class work was Flemish Bond, in which each course consisted of alternate headers and stretchers; this produced an attractively regular finish, and gave scope for decoration if the headers were of a darker colour.

Until the 1740s it was rare for a bricklayer to be called upon to provide more than the basic house walls. On expensive houses embellishments like cornices, pilasters, columns and pediments were almost invariably of stone. It was considered particularly important to have stone blocks to bond the corners securely, and these 'quoins' became a prominent decorative feature of early eighteenth-century houses. More modest town houses of the time, however, show signs of experiment with brick embellishments, such as 'dentillation' — the technique of laying bricks to project in a pattern resembling teeth. (This form of decoration was often used beneath eaves or to provide a string course.) Similarly, brick could be used in preference to expensive stone to produce eaves parapets or distinctive window surrounds;

the latter often featured 'voussoirs' — the finely-crafted wedge-shaped bricks used to form arches.

It must be said, however, that not all brickwork was first-class. The Georgian period is noted for some of the most virtuoso bricklaying ever achieved, but also for some of the most appalling jerry-building. At one extreme the bricklayer could be required to emulate almost anything within the stonemason's repertoire — columns, pilasters, delicate window arches, complex mouldings and sculpture; at the other he could be instructed to cut corners and economise until the structural safety of the building was threatened.

Jerry-building was most common in large-scale urban speculative developments, where cash flow was a constant problem. Savings could be made in various ways. A popular device was to substitute long lengths of cheap timber for courses of bricks on the interior skin of the wall, which would, of course, be plastered over. Another was to cut the header bricks in half, so that while the exterior would apparently consist of impeccable Flemish Bond the two skins would hardly be tied together.

This sort of habit was probably rare in Shropshire, partly because there were no big speculative schemes, but also because builders working on a very local scale had to be careful of their reputations. We should remember, nevertheless, that the majority of Georgian brick structures in the county were built with the utmost economy. The smaller farmhouses, the barns, the

These semi-detached houses at Condover have been skilfully unified by a central pediment over the eaves and over both doors. The two doors have also been given a single case. To complete the illusion a false central window has been inserted on the first floor.

The 'sag' and irregular window shapes of these cottages at Ludlow show the effect of casing a timber-framed structure.

cottages for estate and farm workers, the terraces of artisans' houses, the small shops and the minor industrial buildings were seldom constructed under the close supervision of an architect. Sketchy foundations and economical brick bonding were common in these cases. We have little evidence of the remedial work that must often have been necessary on cheaper structures, although iron ties sometimes provide a hint.

What has been said about new brick buildings applies equally to the very common Georgian habit of applying brick to older structures. This has been discussed elsewhere, but it is worth pointing out again that there were two ways of doing it. The easier and cheaper method was to remove the wattle and daub infilling from a timber frame and replace it with bricks, either in horizontal courses or in a herringbone pattern. This type of refurbishment — brick nogging — can be seen in many farm buildings and also in small village houses given a new lease of life as farmworkers' cottages. In these cases the new walls were usually left exposed, but when town houses were similarly adapted it was usual to smarten them with a coating of plaster, often replaced later by cement rendering.

The second method was to build a new and separate brick façade. This was not so straightforward because the desire was for a 'modern' appearance, with tall sash windows regularly positioned. The old irregular timber frame would rarely fit the new pattern, so it would either be removed completely or drastically adapted. It should be noted that only the façade was affected, so it is common in towns to see houses with elegant brick frontages and their original timber framing on view at the sides and rear. Another necessary operation in this kind of adaptation was the raising of the roof to allow room for the popular two-and-a-half storey façade; this was a fairly simple process of fixing additional timbers to the existing roof structure.

The mortar used in Georgian brickwork was invariably composed of slaked lime and sand; it varied in colour according to the type of sand used, and could complement the colour of the bricks. Portland cement did not become widely available until the 1850s, when its greater strength and weather resistance led to its exclusive use for routine building. In prestigious buildings, however, lime mortar continued to be favoured throughout the nineteenth century because of its superior appearance, and it is still used in high-quality restoration work on Georgian buildings.

The universal use of brick, particularly its use in working-class housing and industrial buildings, produced a reaction in favour of stone in the early nineteenth century. Unfortunately, stone was far too expensive to be used on the majority of buildings; ashlar facing over brick was a cheaper compromise, but the development of 'Roman cement' or stucco made it possible even for modest houses to acquire the appearance of stone. The rendering was applied to the brickwork and then grooved to give the impression of ashlar masonry. This technique is a familiar feature of Regency town houses. For rainproofing purposes the stucco was given several coats of limewash, which produced a 'natural' finish — the modern practice of painting these houses in 'Regency' colours is misconceived.

Building with Stone

The master-masons had been key figures in English building since Saxon times. They were the technical geniuses behind the great ecclesiastical buildings of the Middle Ages and the large mansions of the sixteenth and seventeenth centuries, carrying out most of the functions of architects. Indeed, many stonemasons (Thomas Telford is a famous example) successfully made the transition to architecture during the eighteenth century when there was little formal training, and the new breed of 'gentlemen architects' relied heavily on their technical expertise, even when brick was universally popular.

A large number of skilled under-masons, faced with a decline in their trade, must have become bricklayers, but enough remained to continue the traditions of the craft. Their techniques are described in detail in Volume 2, but in view of the 'stone revival' at the end of the eighteenth century it is useful to outline them again briefly.

The walls of a stone building were constructed as two 'skins', producing something like the modern cavity wall, although in this case the cavity would be packed with small rubble to prevent the two sides from collapsing inwards. At intervals 'tie-stones' would be placed across the double wall to hold the two skins together. In good-class work the stones would be bedded in lime mortar, but elsewhere clay might be used.

Unlike modern non-specialist builders, the masons would never rely on mortar to hold the stones in place; what kept the walls stable was the skill that went into the laying of the stones so that they bonded firmly together under their own weight. The main virtue of mortar or mud was that it provided a form of draughtproofing.

The stone the mason was working with could arrive in various forms, depending on the quality of the job. Good building stone will usually break out in the quarry with at least one straight side, but it might have been given additional 'dressing' to provide a presentable external face. On cheaper jobs he might be expected to 'face' each stone roughly as he used it, a process that was not too difficult with the Shropshire limestones and sandstones. For the most expensive work the stones for the external face would be shaped and squared to a uniform size at the quarry.

Stone-laying technique depended entirely on the nature of the stone, and two main methods were used. 'Ashlar' masonry involved the use of stones cut to identical size and precise right angles. The result was the very superior appearance of uniform rectangular stones laid in perfectly level courses and with very thin mortar joints, but it was highly expensive and the same effect was often obtained by laying thin vertical slabs over a main structure of brick or irregular stonework.

The use of stucco during the Regency period to give the illusion of ashlar masonry has already been described.

In less expensive work the usual technique was to lay the stones in their natural shapes and sizes, a method known as 'rubble masonry'. (This term did not necessarily denote inferior work — after all, many of the great ecclesiastical buildings of the Middle Ages involved rubble construction.) If the material permitted, it was usual to attempt 'coursed rubble' laying, where the stones would be selected for height, set in rough horizontal courses and levelled off occasionally with flat pieces. Where the stones showed no uniformity of size or shape a 'random rubble' technique would be used, with the stones laid wherever they fitted best and with no attempt at coursing.

Rubble masonry can be seen on the hundreds of Shropshire farmhouses

The market hall at Clun is typical of several built in the county towards the end of the eighteenth century. It is of rubble construction with ashlar dressings. The ground floor was originally open, and the first floor would have been used for civic purposes.

and cottages that were built or cased in stone during the eighteenth century. There are particularly good examples in the Wenlock Edge/Corvedale area; Hungerford Farm near Munslow proves that skilful rubble construction could produce a refined and imposing effect, and there is a magnificent rubble stone house in Broad Street, Ludlow. Sandstone breaks out in large pieces that are quite easily given a rough square shape, and the Baschurch/Ruyton area is particularly rich in examples of its use during the eighteenth century for cottages and small houses. Sometimes the blocks seem grotesquely large for the size of the building.

Coursed work was always preferred because it produced more secure bonding. The essential thing was to bond the stones laterally and longitudinally. Lateral bonding was achieved by using tie stones and by laying stones with their length into the wall so that they were firmly locked into place by the weight on top of them. Longitudinal bonding depended on each joint between stones being covered by a stone on the top as in brickwork, and this was always easier to achieve by the use of regular courses. Failure to do it resulted in vertical cracks along which the stones could 'burst'.

This exceptionally fine house in Broad Street, Ludlow, is by T. F. Pritchard and illustrates several popular structural devices of the mid-eighteenth century. Unusually for a large town house it is faced with coursed rubble limestone. The centre bay is brought forward and embellished by an eaves pediment, an enriched first-floor window and a dignified entrance with pilasters and a 'broken' pediment. The hipped roof with dormers went out of fashion later in the century.

In houses built in rubble masonry the potential weak points are at the angles and in the openings for doors and windows. For this reason the mason would select special long stones and shape them into rectangular form and uniform size to give strength and neatness to the corners. The same technique was used in miniature at door and window jambs, leading to various kinds of decorative treatment.

These techniques were part of the mason's basic training, but he was often called upon to demonstrate skills of a higher order. The seventeenth century had seen the introduction of increasingly strange and complex work, such as classical columns, pilasters, elaborate cornices or balustraded parapets. Although showy stone dressings declined in popularity among people of fashion during the eighteenth century, they remained popular lower down the social scale, and even very modest brick villas in town or country would at least have stone embellishments to their doors and windows. In this respect the mason's task was made easier by the large number of 'pattern books' available, providing designs from which the client could choose. Inevitably many masons ceased to work directly on buildings and specialised instead in supplying decorative features.

General Building Technology

Before 1700 it was still quite rare in Shropshire to find a house more than one room deep, since the depth was decided by the maximum length of timber that would stretch between the exterior walls. One important result of the widespread availability of brick was that it made load-bearing interior walls possible for a wide range of houses, and the double-pile house, two rooms deep, became the norm for all but the very cheapest dwellings.

Thus the standard practice of the period, suiting the taste for symmetry, was to stack pairs of rooms of identical size on top of each other. The typical large double-fronted (three-bay) house of the later eighteenth century would have four rooms on each floor, divided by entrance hall, staircase and landings. In a semi-detached or terraced house there would be two rooms on each floor with the staircase placed on one side.

The fashion for very low, unobtrusive roofs ruled out the possibility of garrets with dormers — an arrangement very popular in the early eighteenth century. In most Georgian houses servants were accommodated in attic dormitories forming a half-storey at the top of the house. Town residences normally had their kitchens and other service rooms located in a basement, sometimes reached by an 'area' — a space at the front of the house below street level, providing access and some daylight — although this practice was not always adopted in country houses, where there would be ample room for a service block or wing at the rear.

The most obvious common feature of Georgian and Regency houses is, of course, their small-paned sash windows, which first appeared as a luxury fitting at the end of the seventeenth century. In the early years of their use they had thick glazing bars and were normally fitted flush with the outside wall. By the mid-eighteenth century they were being installed in a recess of at least four inches, largely as a result of urban building regulations to minimise

The Venetian window was a feature of Palladian architecture that persisted throughout the eighteenth century. Normally it would occupy the centre bay on the first floor, but the builder of this house in Ludlow had other ideas.

the spread of fire. As the century progressed glazing bars became thinner, and the ultra-slender bars of Regency houses contribute much to the elegance of their windows. Trying to date a building by its windows, however, is an uncertain business because they were the items most frequently replaced as fashions changed.

The casement window survived in small cottages, and occasionally it is possible to find the older lateral sliding window still intact (a cottage in Willow Street, Oswestry, has them). On the whole these earlier types were a better proposition for cased timber-framed houses, where it was not always possible to set windows to the accurate vertical necessary for the easy movement of sashes.

Doorcases were very important to Georgian houseowners since they often provided the only major embellishment to the façade. The taste of the early eighteenth century had been for pilasters on each side of the door and a hood over the top. Frequently these hoods would be designed to resemble a shell — an attractive feature that has all but disappeared in Shropshire, although there are examples in St John's Street, Bridgnorth, and Green End, Whitchurch.

Hoods provided minimal cover, and it may have been for purely practical reasons that the fashion for larger covered porches developed. Whatever the reason, they rapidly became universally popular even on very small houses where their columns and pediments can seem incongruous today.

The principles governing the 'Orders' used in these and other classical features are described at the end of Part Two.

Part Five
Looking at Buildings: The Towns

Bishop's Castle

The long main street is notable for some remarkable cased timber-framing, especially in Market Square and the antique shop opposite the Town Hall. Other good examples are No. 27 High Street (spectacularly warped) and No. 64, which has extraordinarily wide-set windows. At the southern end of the town No. 7 Church Street is a good early eighteenth-century house, and almost opposite are Nos. 16-18, a late-Georgian semi-detached pair with none of the usual attempts at unification. The Town Hall (c. 1765) is built on the steepest part of the hill in red brick with quoins and a rusticated stone basement that was once the gaol — hence the small circular windows. Above them is a first-floor Venetian window. On the main street frontage is a row of unusually wide round-headed windows with embellished iron glazing bars that are no doubt of later date.

Bridgnorth

Although Bridgnorth derived considerable prosperity from the river trade and from industry during the eighteenth century, it was never a fashionable town like Shrewsbury or Ludlow, so one would not expect outstanding buildings of the period. There are a few distinguished houses, but the town is notable mainly for a remarkable variety of homelier domestic architecture, much of it dating from the early nineteenth century before economic decline began to set in.

The older part of Low Town, and Mill Street in particular, is full of interest, with a range of façades spanning several centuries. There are many examples here of brick-cased timber frames of the eighteenth century and one or two distinctive early nineteenth-century frontages, for instance Nos. 11 and 46-47. The Foster's Arms has shallow bow windows characteristic of the Regency period, and so has No. 1 Bridge Street. Facing Mill Street is the rambling Falcon Hotel, a coaching inn smartened up in the early 1800s but with leaning windows that betray the timber frame behind the façade.

Bridge Street continues as St John's Street, and at the far end is a very big house of uncertain date. It has a conventional Georgian three-bay front, but there are three full storeys instead of the usual two-and-a-half, and the roof is steeply pitched with dormers. Elsewhere in Bridgnorth there are indications of a local attachment to this old-fashioned feature in preference to the more usual flatter roof with a low attic storey beneath it. To confuse matters further, the house has a magnificent shell hood over its door — a feature more common in the early eighteenth century. From here there is a view across the A422 of a row of early nineteenth-century villas, differing slightly in their details but forming quite a unified terrace.

The old wharf area is on the other side of the bridge, and among the remaining buildings is an interesting symmetrical composition of the early nineteenth century, consisting of two three-storey blocks with a lower section between them. The outer 'wings' each have three blind arches on their faces, containing a variety of round-headed windows, while the central section has two entrance bays, each pedimented and with keystoned arches to the doors. Again, there is a variety of windows, some of them modern. The Severn Arms Hotel has a frontage of the same period with a Victorian bay window added.

From the wharf Cartway leads up into High Town. Bridgnorth's High Street is a fine architectural mix of exposed timber-frames, later brick casings and more recent façades, but there are few outstanding Georgian buildings. However, it is worth exploring the side roads to the west. St Mary's Street has a good example at No. 62 of what might be called the typical Georgian town house — very plain, three bays and two-and-a-half storeys. Nos. 18-19 are a semi-detached pair, unified by a central passageway and by a central first-floor window (presumably the first-floor rooms interlock so that the other house has a corresponding window at the back). At the bottom of the street is a very imposing three-bay house, again completely plain apart from what is probably a later porch.

Whitburn Street also has an interesting group at its far end, including a row of urban cottages with frontages that appear to be of about 1800. Next to them is No. 33, a double-fronted cottage of the same period with dormers. The tall house opposite is a reminder of the Baroque style of the early eighteenth century, featuring heavily-decorated eaves, a string course and prominent quoins. Again, the porch is an addition, an attempt at simple modernisation later in the century. Another, and better, example of pre-Georgian Baroque can be seen back in the High Street, where Northgate House is tucked away at the extreme northern end. It illustrates clearly the showiness that was so quickly discarded in the mid-eighteenth century.

The almshouses in Church Street, to the north, are instructive in their ugliness. Dated 1792, they have seven bays with a pediment over the centre three. Access is by a central passageway. Their mean appearance is explained by the fact that they were a municipal enterprise; most other almshouses in the county were founded by private individuals who took care to perpetuate their names with buildings of some aesthetic value. At the top of Church Street the little close that surrounds St Leonard's provides further examples of the abiding popularity in Bridgnorth of steep-pitched roofs and dormers. Nos. 26-27 are semi-detached and unusual in having no form of unification. The big isolated building nearby is notable mainly for a wide variety of windows — Venetian, round-headed and rectangular are freely mixed.

The southern end of the town can be reached by walking back through the High Street, but a pleasant alternative is to descend St Leonard's Steps into the Cartway and to climb St Mary's Steps from the wharf. This provides an opportunity to see some of the humbler cottages behind and below the main streets. When St Mary's Steps join Castle Hill Walk a change of atmosphere can be felt at once. This was the fashionable end of town, and the Walk around the castle was constructed in the late eighteenth century to allow polite recreation and to afford a spectacular view of the Severn valley.

St Mary's Church, Bridgnorth, by Thomas Telford.

The focal point here is Telford's church of St Mary Magdalene. Designed in 1792 to dominate the promontory once occupied by the castle, it looks bigger than it is, an effect helped by an imposing attached portico on the entrance front. This has massive pilasters on the outside and Tuscan columns within. On the walls of the rectangular nave pairs of pilasters alternate with huge round-headed windows of clear glass in thin glazing bars. The tower, rising from a square base, has an elaborate first stage featuring a sequence of columns and pilasters surmounted by a cornice, while the second stage consists of a dome on a polygonal base. Within the church Telford's original concept of clear white light can still be appreciated, although his design for a simple rectangle containing nave and chancel was destroyed in 1876 when the taste for a 'mystery' around the altar led to the addition of an apse suitably darkened by stained glass. Unusually for this type of church there is a single small gallery at the west end, allowing an uncluttered interior in which the two giant colonnades can make their full effect.

The only road to the church is East Castle Street, Bridgnorth's fashionable eighteenth-century thoroughfare. The oldest building here is No. 18, the Governor's House of 1633, and it decided the building line of the street. Outstanding individual houses here include No. 16, with its four Venetian windows and No. 15, a three-bay house with the central bay pedimented and strongly emphasised by brick pilaster strips. Further along on the left are some examples of houses in polychrome brick, a device that could sometimes give an 'industrial' effect, but which succeeds here because the houses vary in size and design. Beyond the Governor's House is an unbroken row of harmonious middle-class residences and, again, dormer windows are very much in evidence at quite a late date. No. 26 ends the sequence — a conventional Georgian town house, but built with quoins long after they had gone out of fashion.

A final look back along East Castle Street, closed off by the church, provides a vista of airy Georgian streetscape that perhaps only Ludlow can match.

Ellesmere

Ellesmere's Georgian architecture is homely rather than distinguished, but the wide variety of styles gives the town a considerable charm.

Perhaps the best place to start a walk is in Church Street, which looks like a select eighteenth-century suburb but which was in fact the original market place. At the Mere end No. 25 is a big three-bay house with a central eaves pediment (a popular feature in Ellesmere) and a cornice decorated with dentillated brick. The doorway is surprisingly insignificant, but even at that time space beside the road would have been restricted. Nos. 23 and 21 are in a single block, very plain and with round-headed windows. No. 17 is detached and has rather cramped proportions; again the main feature is an eaves pediment. On the opposite side the Red Lion is no doubt older than its early Victorian façade suggests, but any character it may have is swamped beneath

These two houses in East Castle Street, Bridgnorth, show that popular eighteenth-century embellishments could be used naively by urban builders. The nearer house is badly-proportioned and features Venetian windows fitted indiscriminately, while the house in the background has an outsize central eaves pediment.

gaudy pub trappings. Standing opposite the end of Watergate Street is a well-proportioned four-bay house with a very handsome front door.

In Watergate Street the buildings are predominantly small-scale shops and cottages, but two prominent houses face each other. One is evidently of the later eighteenth century, in brick with imposing ground-floor windows, while the other has a rusticated ashlar facing typical of the early nineteenth century. Both have an identical two-and-a-half storey design.

A few yards further on, a left turn brings you into St John's Hill, Ellesmere's most attractive street, where a row of old houses with late Georgian façades ascends steeply. At the bottom, No. 6 is extraordinarily tall and thin. It may be that it was originally part of its neighbour, which has been transformed into a three-bay symmetrical house with a naive façade featuring much blank brick. Nos. 12 and 10 are of interest because they are semi-detached, and an attempt has been made to give them importance by placing a single pediment over their doors. The row is completed by some attractive cottages that suggest interior timber-framing. Opposite them a lane leads to The Mount, a severe rectangle, imposing because of its high position and in the same basic style as the Church Street houses.

Back in the short High Street the ground floors have all been altered by the insertion of shop fronts, but the first floors reveal an attractive variety of Georgian styles. The Bridgewater Arms was a traditional eighteenth-century coaching inn before its early Victorian remodelling. The next outstanding building is the old Town Hall, a unique structure of the 1830s. Its rusticated ashlar front, immense windows and giant eaves pediment give it great presence in the narrow street.

Cross Street now continues as Scotland Street, and immediately noticeable on the right is the remarkable façade of the Black Lion. Long and low, it appears to be early nineteenth century, although the strange assembly of features confuses the issue. Both the eaves cornice and the string course are decorated with modillions, while all the upstairs windows have their own heavy cornices with scroll brackets. The centre first-floor window is ornamented in no known style. The whole effect is pleasantly eccentric. Much more discipline is apparent in the old Savings Bank further up on the left; it dates from about 1820, and its chaste Grecian dignity was intended to inspire confidence. Unfortunately, a large shop window has spoilt the façade. At the extreme end of Scotland Street, on a sharp bend is a decaying house that is difficult to date. Its porch has five columns, one of which supports a small turret, and this work appears to be mid-Victorian. The side, however, suggests a Regency date, with its delicate iron balcony and verandah.

Victoria Street leads off Scotland Street, and the prominent building here is Fullwood House, now the library. This is contemporary with the Savings Bank, and is similarly designed to impress, with its important porch on four columns and its striking round-arch embellishment on the first floor. The same device is used to mark out the ground-floor windows. The road continues as Willow Street, and contains several interesting buildings of the period, including two pleasingly simple villas of the 1830s and another pair of Georgian semi-detached houses given unity and symmetry by a shared pediment over their doors.

Finally, where Victoria Street ends in a roundabout, comes Ellesmere's best feature — Charlotte Row, a long terrace of artisans' cottages dating from the 1830s. Modernisation has removed most of the original doors and windows, but the cottages have not become gentrified, and the owners still keep up the tradition of vegetable-growing in their long front gardens.

Ellesmere's canal buildings are described in Part Three.

Ludlow

Ludlow has some fine individual buildings of the period, but of all the Shropshire towns it demonstrates most strikingly the harmonious streetscapes that resulted from the architecture of the later eighteenth and early nineteenth centuries. The effect of Broad Street and Mill Street is to make us aware of the agreeable environment produced by a combination of wealth and taste, and these two thoroughfares have rightly become showpieces. Nevertheless, from the point of view of urban development the more interesting area is Corve Street, and it is useful to start a walk at its lower end.

Lower Corve Street, now cut off by a new road, contains a wealth of timber-framed buildings that must once have been the end of a long development away from the town centre during the sixteenth and seventeenth centuries. Some of the houses here were later brick-cased without losing their original character, but as we move up Corve Street we begin to see the process of complete remodelling in accordance with formal fashion.

Actually, the first building of note is a piece of startling innovation. The Stone House, now the offices of South Shropshire District Council, is a most sophisticated façade of about 1840, perhaps the best example in the county of the transition between the tastes of the eighteenth century and the Victorian period. Giant pilasters had been out of fashion for a hundred years, but here they return as a way of articulating the façade. They are used with restraint — suggested rather than emphasised. The house has the conventional three bays and two-and-a-half storeys, but added importance is conferred by a very high eaves cornice and parapet. The enrichment of the first-floor windows with pediments and console brackets is not repeated on the ground floor, where the emphasis is firmly on the porch, which relies on mass rather than decoration for its effect.

Further up on the right, the wide façade of No. 28 is basically naive, but boasts a Venetian window and a fanlight. Nos. 11 and 10, also on the right, are an interesting pair; the former is a big five-bay house with a pedimented and fanlighted doorway, while the latter is on a smaller scale but a complete match in style. Who copied whom? Nos. 9 and 8 are semi-detached and unified by the placing of the two doors side by side, but this is likely to have been a late adaptation — the style of the doors does not match the older façade above, and an extra wing has been awkwardly tacked on, perhaps to overcome the problem of converting a five-bay house into two.

On the opposite side of the road is a row of cased timber frames demonstrating an easier and less expensive way of modernising, but a little way up from them No. 145 stands out as an elegant piece of work, with five bays but only two storeys. There is a very plain pedimented door and apparently two blind windows.

In walking from the top of Corve Street through King Street we plunge suddenly into the huddle of the town's commercial centre. Narrow plots and modest incomes gave little opportunity for ambitious remodelling, and renovation was confined to the casing of existing façades. In the middle of all this the Butter Cross comes as a surprise, but it must have been positively startling when it was built in the 1740s, a classical intrusion into a medieval streetscape. At that time, of course, Broad Street was already becoming fashionable, and the new Town Hall was consciously sited to close it off at the top. It is a three-bay structure with a semi-circular first-floor window, a balustrade and cupola, but the dominant feature is the porch — four-columned and pedimented, a miniature portico.

Moving past it towards the castle we enter the Square, much more deserving of the name since the demolition of the Victorian town hall. There are two impressive buildings of the period here. Adjoining the castle gate, Ludlow College occupies a huge five-bay structure, apparently of the early nineteenth century but with odd features that must surely be the result of adaptation for school use. On the ground floor pairs of close-set windows on each side of the porch strike a jarring note, while another huge window has been set into the eaves. Directly opposite, at the top of Mill Street, are the former Assembly Rooms of 1840, very dignified in a Regency-influenced style and embellished with giant pilasters similar to those on the Stone House in Corve Street. The annexe in Mill Street has a pediment with Ionic pilasters.

Dinham Hall, Ludlow, is severe and stone-built, exemplifying the influence of the Greek Revival movement of the early nineteenth century.

Dinham, leading off the south-west corner of the Square, is a street of great charm. Ludlow lacks distinctive Regency architecture, but No. 7 Dinham provides a small taste, with an attractive balcony and hooded window on the side and an oriel window on the street front, which actually hides a much older house. Close by is Dinham Hall, an austere ashlar-faced house of the early nineteenth century; its rather rugged effect is emphasised by the stone surround to its door. The door of No. 11 has a Shropshire rarity — a 'Gibbs surround'. This design of spaced blocks linked by vertical bands, with voussoirs in the arch, was popularised early in the eighteenth century by James Gibbs, architect of St Martin-in-the-Fields. This house also has unusually emphatic keystones on its windows. Its neighbour has a similar façade but plain windows and an Ionic doorway.

The nine-bay frontage of Dinham House dominates the next corner. Its design, with projecting end bays and garrets above the eaves parapet, shows the influence of the early eighteenth century before the fashion for incorporating the attic storey into the façade. Its neighbour, Dinham Lodge, has the two-and-a-half storey arrangement and is perfectly conventional, apart from its round-headed porch flanked by very unorthodox columns, possibly an early nineteenth-century modification.

A walk down to the river from here is justified by the view of the castle, but it also provides an opportunity to look at Dinham bridge (1825), a structure of three broad arches embellished with unusual half-round pilasters.

Camp Lane branches off from Dinham and joins the bottom of Mill Street, which is an excellent illustration of the near-static architectural taste of provincial citizens in the eighteenth century. The houses here probably span a hundred years of 'Georgian' building, but this is hardly evident at first glance. Closer inspection reveals the differences between the rougher brickwork and segment-headed windows of early houses like No. 55 and the greater sophistication of No. 41, but the total effect is one of unity and of a conservatism that makes it impossible to pick out individual houses for comment.

The same cannot be said for Broad Street, where idiosyncratic details exist without spoiling the prevailing harmony. At the top, for example, the timber-framed Angel Hotel acquired a pair of Regency bow windows. Further down, No. 18 originally had a conventional five-bay façade and columned porch, but it had not been up very long before it was divided, with a second, smaller door being clumsily forced in at one side. Almost opposite is No. 49, a former inn transformed in the early nineteenth century and given a very wide porch with a keystoned arch and Ionic pilasters.

Back on the left-hand side, No. 27 is a most striking house, reputedly by T. F. Pritchard. Built on a generous scale, it is faced with pale grey limestone more familiar on country houses in the Much Wenlock area, and follows the mid-eighteenth century fashion for emphasising the middle bay, in this case by means of a tripartite pedimented doorway and an enriched round-headed window above. The final group on the right-hand side forms an interesting terrace dating from quite early in the period. No. 39 has long been famous (or notorious) for the eccentric taste of its builder, who insisted on Venetian windows for the entire frontage. Below it are two conventional five-bay

Early nineteenth-century cottages at Market Drayton.

houses with the usual pediments and pilasters at their doors. The bottom pair must be of very early date, since they share the kind of steep-pitched roof with dormers popular in the Queen Anne period. Their fanlighted doors were no doubt fitted a hundred years or so later.

The street is closed off by the Broad Gate, a medieval structure curiously converted into a castellated house in the mid-eighteenth century. It makes no pretence at regularity, though there is no way of telling whether this was the result of a desire for picturesqueness or simply the difficulty of fitting the house into an awkward space.

Before leaving this area it is worth walking through Bell Lane, which has several good examples of brick-faced timber-framed cottages, and Brand Lane, where there are some surprisingly good Georgian houses, including the impressive seven-bay Brand House.

Market Drayton

The main streets of Market Drayton lead away from the High Street, which forms a central square. Here the outstanding building of the period is the Corbet Arms, a coaching inn of three very wide bays with a columned and pedimented porch.

Great Hales Street runs to the east, and almost opposite the garage is Rylands House, included in the previous volume but worth inspecting again as an early forerunner of Georgian style. A little further along on the left is a pair of small and very attractive semi-detached villas of the early nineteenth century. Their porches have console brackets and fluted columns made of wood, and the bay windows are topped with bracketed cornices.

In Cheshire Street, to the west of the High Street, stands the Buttercross, an open market hall of 1824 consisting of little more than a shallow pitched roof with bell turret, supported on fourteen Tuscan columns (some replaced).

The most interesting buildings of the period are in Shropshire Street to the south. They include the Red House opposite the junction with Frogmore Road — an impressively wide seven-bay mansion with an added wing that upsets the symmetry. The centre three bays project under an eaves pediment and the flat-headed windows have the large keystone popular on many local houses. Note the unobtrusive brick quoins. The fine front door has attached fluted columns and an enriched pediment. No. 39 is less grand but a good example of the sort of solid house built by successful professional men in the eighteenth century. No. 41 belongs to the very beginning of the century and makes a useful contrast with the Red House — far from hiding its roof the builder emphasised it with two plain dormers and a centre one incorporated into a shaped gable. The basement, which has the effect of raising the principal floor well above street level, was to become a standard feature of later town houses.

Much Wenlock

Any traveller on the A458 can hardly fail to notice the town's most striking Georgian building. The Gaskell Arms, a sprawling roadside inn, is basically of much earlier date, but the façade was remodelled in the hey-day of the stage-coach to provide an unusually wide frontage of five broad bays and two low storeys. The pilastered doorway is surmounted by a semi-circular arch containing a fanlight, while the canted bay windows (the upper slightly taller than the lower) are topped off with a kind of half-dome. The early nineteenth-century house opposite (now clad in grey roughcast) has a conventional double front with canted bays, but the four giant pilasters add an idiosyncratic touch. In Bourton Road, to the south-west of the inn, is a big and rather gaunt brick house, demonstrating the continuing popularity of the hipped roof in Shropshire long after it ceased to be fashionable. Further up Bourton Road, 'Greenfields' is a prim early nineteenth-century villa with an unusual type of segmental window-head found elsewhere in the town, and evidently the whim of a local builder.

In the other direction the High Street leads into the town centre. The street has a good many eighteenth-century cottages, either new or refaced. From the Square it is worth walking along Barrow Street. Nos. 13-14 are typical small villas built to different scales but sharing the same window designs. No. 12 is probably the most impressive Georgian private house in the town, with four wide bays and big sixteen-light windows. On the other side of the road No. 29 is an interesting former shop building with the small-paned bow windows typical of the Regency period. St Mary's Lane leads uphill off Barrow Street and contains an outstanding example of a small cottage in the Gothick style, with pointed windows and a prominent 'Jacobean' gable.

To the north of the Square Wilmore Street reveals some unremarkable eighteenth-century work, and in the Bull Ring is the well-preserved Savings Bank — a very characteristic building of 1829 featuring a handsome doorcase

Patterned brick on houses in East Castle Street, Bridgnorth. (The house in the foreground has been remodelled. The attic windows show that it was once a conventional Georgian house of three bays and two-and-a-half storeys. One of the original first-floor windows remains, but the two large windows and the re-set door are Victorian.)

Brogyntyn Hall, near Oswestry. Originally a provincial Baroque house of the early 1700s, it was completely remodelled externally in the early nineteenth century to conform to the new Greek Revival taste. A very elaborate Ionic portico dominates the façade.

St Chad's, Shrewsbury, by George Steuart — Shropshire's finest eighteenth-century church.

Maesbury Marsh, showing the wharf and the Navigation Inn.

The large windows and wealth of decorative ironwork at The Lyth, Ellesmere, demonstrate the combination of relaxed taste and elegance associated with the Regency period.

Stone House, Corve Street, Ludlow — an example of the transition in architecture between Georgian correctness and Victorian freedom.

with fanlight and the type of window-head previously noted in Bourton Road. Finally, in Shineton Street the Wolmer's Almshouses of about 1810 are another example of restrained Gothick taste.

Newport

Newport is the most Georgian town in Shropshire, but so unobtrusive is the architecture that it is difficult to find a building of outstanding merit. A walk along the High Street will reveal any number of façades in a variety of naive styles that have no pretensions to grandeur — indeed, an unusually high proportion have the 'wavy' look that indicate a brick front to a timber frame, and this can often be confirmed by a glance down the many side passages.

One point of interest at the extreme northern end of the High Street is the wharf area of the waterway which was opened in 1835 to link the Shrewsbury Canal with the Birmingham and Liverpool Canal, the junction being at Norbury to the north-east of Newport. Apart from a lock chamber, very little survives.

Walking from here into the town centre you pass on your right a row of eighteenth-century buildings of varying degrees of grandeur. In the centre is Beaumaris House, a distinguished structure of 1724. Its neighbour, Roddam House, cannot be much later, and they both feature the prominent keystones seen on so many buildings in Newport. Almost opposite Beaumaris House is the Rectory, and there could hardly be a better example of a small, dignified

The Royal Victoria Hotel, Newport, a very dignified structure of c. 1830, with its centre three bays emphasised by an eaves pediment and giant pilasters.

town residence of the early nineteenth century — very plain apart from its porch with four Ionic columns. Note the characteristic carriage sweep.

At the point where the road divides around the church the Royal Victoria Hotel stands out splendidly. Dating from the 1830s, it has the fashionable five bays and two-and-a-half storeys surmounted by a very shallow pediment. A series of pilasters decorate the first floor, while the ground floor has rusticated stucco work. Past the church the High Street is lined with buildings of a homelier kind, but it is worth studying Barclay's Bank opposite the big Victorian Town Hall. It is an odd design, no doubt a fanciful piece of early nineteenth-century work, consisting of a Georgian façade with a subdued doorway but a first-floor centre window richly framed by a semi-circular arch supported on Ionic columns. It has the look of a former inn.

Oswestry

Like all Shropshire towns, Oswestry has plenty of Georgian and early Victorian architecture of what might be called the workaday kind — a mixture of shops, short terraces, villas and cottages — but among them are several distinctive buildings of great interest.

A good starting-point is Upper Brook Street at its junction with Welsh Walls. The tall, narrow houses opposite the junction have been mentioned in the previous volume, but it is worth pointing out again that they represent a very crude attempt in the 1720s to create the kind of house that had become popular in larger towns — a brick façade to a timber structure, with the new sash windows (very tall and narrow here because of the house dimensions). On the same side a few yards down the street is a sophisticated contrast. It is a late eighteenth-century scheme demonstrating a unified treatment of two pairs of semi-detached houses with a centre passage. Its symmetry is difficult to grasp at first because of varied paintwork and an obtrusive Victorian bay window. The outstanding design feature is the provision of wide, segment-headed windows with an unusual fan design above them.

In Lower Brook Street, beyond the traffic lights, there are further interesting contrasts. No. 6 is a three-bay, two-storey mid-Georgian house in dark brick, proving that the taste for the much earlier Queen Anne style lingered in the less fashionable towns. Its steep pitched roof, attic dormers and prominent quoins had long become obsolete elsewhere. The keystones in the window arches are the only 'new' feature. The adjoining house was apparently refaced in the ashlar stone popular in the early nineteenth century. No. 12 is dated 1741, but resembles No. 6 in its disregard for newer fashions. In fact this is an exceptionally handsome façade, with the odd omission of a front door. Prominent on the other side of the road is a short terrace combining an impressive town house and a pair of semi-detached villas, all later Georgian. The interesting feature of the large house is the brick parapet incorporating blind balustrades.

In Church Street the eye is taken immediately by the Wynnstay Hotel, refashioned in the early nineteenth century in a style typical of staging inns all over the country. Modern bits and pieces detract from the plain dignity of the façade, but the big, welcoming porch survives, supported over the pavement on columns. Almost directly opposite is Bellan House, easily the most impressive house of the period in Oswestry. Hardly recognisable as late Georgian, its design is dominated by immense two-storey bays on each side of a comparatively insignificant, though beautifully-crafted, entrance. There are eaves pediments over each bay, and the attic storey is virtually invisible. A few yards along the street it is easy to overlook the fact that the two modest houses on each side of the park gates are twins. On the same side and near the Cross is The Old Vaults, a pub with an attractive early nineteenth-century frontage like that of a shop, with its large ground floor windows.

Willow Street, leading away from Church Street at the Cross, has several Georgian town residences at its lower end, and at the junction with Welsh Walls Nos. 63-65 are good examples of the small villas of the later eighteenth century, one of them having an elaborate window case. Porkington Terrace, at the top of Willow Street, should not be missed. It is the handsomest terrace in the town — five double-fronted villas built in 1840 and unified by a slight projection of the eaves cornice over the centre house. The railings of their private pavement survived the war, and they seem to have their original rainwater heads. Finally, just before the Greyhound pub, is a pair of tiny artisans' cottages, one of them as near to the original as you are likely to find nowadays. Both retain their sliding casement windows.

The other buildings of interest are rather more scattered. At the top of Chapel Street, at the entrance to the Horsemarket, is an intriguing pair of small semi-detached houses, probably of the early nineteenth century. They are of three storeys, including a basement reached by area steps (an unusual

This house in Lower Brook Street, Oswestry, illustrates the tendency in less fashionable towns to modify Georgian 'correctness'. Individualistic features here include a bullseye window, stone quoins and a balustraded roof parapet.

feature in Oswestry). The two entrance doors are placed within a big porch with pilasters and columns, giving the impression of a single house. In Arthur Street, close by, is the impressive building of 1830 that was once the Congregational chapel. It has the usual tall, round-headed windows on both floors, and the pedimented front features a big porch with fluted Doric columns.

At the top of Bailey Street, the George Hotel retains much of its mid-eighteenth-century appearance in spite of slick Dickensian renovation. The seven-bay street façade has very prominent quoins and eaves modillions, but the array of console brackets at street level were no doubt added later in the century.

Finally, the east side of Salop Road reveals some interesting speculative developments of the early nineteenth century. The terrace is continuous, but close inspection shows three different schemes for modest middle-class housing. The upper group have later bay windows of elaborate design, and at the other end Nos. 26-30 have particularly rich doorcases.

Lower down, on the other side of Middleton Road, is a semi-detached composition that repeats a design found at the top of the row — the pair are unified by placing an eaves pediment over the two entrance doors. It is dated 1840, but is an interesting throwback to an older taste. The bay windows were added later to conform to the Victorian villa fashion.

Shifnal

Shifnal occupied a strategic position on the London—Shrewsbury road in the eighteenth century, and its importance grew in the early 1800s when improvements to the Holyhead Road brought an increase in stage-coach traffic. One looks in vain, however, for obvious signs of the town's Georgian history. A certain amount of demolition and reconstruction has taken place in the town centre, and the interesting buildings of the period are now scattered fairly widely.

For a lesson in architectural history it is worth starting in Park Street, where Idsall House occupies a prominent site set back from the road. It was included in the previous volume as one of the earliest examples in Shropshire of urban 'provincial Baroque', the debased form of Renaissance design that was becoming fashionable in country districts in the earliest years of the eighteenth century. Dated 1699, it shows off its symmetry, its string course, quoins and keystones as modish status symbols.

For an instructive contrast go to the end of Church Street. Innage House, just beyond the church, has the more modest look of what has become known as 'Queen Anne' style, with its three bays and two-and-a-half storeys, its neat, steep-pitched roof and embellishment confined to a plain eaves cornice and the usual pedimented entrance. Opposite the church porch the Vicarage goes a stage further, and is a classic Georgian urban house — five bays, with the centre bay heavily emphasised by an eaves pediment and enriched window surrounds. There are unobtrusive brick pilaster strips at the corners, and the door has a fanlight, pediment and attached fluted columns. Unusually, the ground floor windows on the entrance front were bricked up.

Also in Church Street, nearer the town centre, are some pleasant terraced villas, probably of the early nineteenth century, then Offley House. This is an attractive example of a gentleman's small town residence of the same period, set back with a short drive behind iron railings.

Apart from Idsall House, Park Street has one or two other buildings of interest. Almost opposite the Nell Gwynne is a timber-framed house that has been given a new brick façade — one among many, but particularly obvious here because of the tell-tale drunken windows. Towards the end of the street a Georgian stable block with small semi-circular windows and the usual cupola has been converted for residential use. The coach arch to the street has been bricked up but survives on the other side. The adjacent Park House Hotel has been smartened up and is now difficult to date, but the porch supported by paired fluted columns is typical of the Regency period.

To the north of the railway bridge Park Street continues as Broadway, and at the further end a number of eighteenth-century houses survive, although the various alterations they have undergone make them of lesser interest. Perhaps the most striking feature here is the group of modern buildings designed to blend with Georgian surroundings.

In Shrewsbury Road there is a strange house next to the old fire station. Dated 1830, it has a conventional three-bay façade, but is only one room deep. Further along the road some small artisans' cottages, no doubt very early Victorian, have survived — one or two virtually unscathed by modernisation.

The area of flat, arable land to the south of Shifnal was prosperous farming country during the late eighteenth century, and it is dotted with good examples of large farmhouses of the period. Beside the A4169 halfway between Shifnal and Madeley is The Hem, with some splendid brick barns.

Shrewsbury

We saw in the previous volume that by 1730 Shrewsbury was beginning to acquire a collection of houses in the new formal style inspired by the Renaissance. The Guildhall, Bowdler's House, the Judges' Lodgings, Hardwick House, Abbeydale House and Abbey House show the new fashion with varying degrees of ambition. As the eighteenth century proceeded, it saw the development of streets and terraces of stylish new housing, particularly on the western side of the town towards the Quarry. At the same time a large number of the old timber-framed houses in the crowded town centre were remodelled or simply refaced in brick to conform to changing tastes. Even the castle received a Georgian treatment.

Confronted with so much building of the period, it is possible to pick out for special mention only what is of distinctive interest or significance. Certainly our starting point, in Howard Street behind the station, is significant because this was the terminus of the Shrewsbury Canal (described in Part Three). What remains of the enterprise, designed to bring cheap coal to the town from the Shropshire coalfield, is a magnificent warehouse, now known as the Buttermarket. Dating from 1835 it has the Grecian look considered suitable then for serious public buildings, with an entrance façade consisting of a huge entrance porch flanked by massive Doric columns. On each side are symmetrical wings (one slightly skewed), with three round-headed windows and pediments on the outer bays. The side elevation is more utilitarian, in plain brick and with a sack hoist, but even here there are elegant windows and pediments.

A few yards further up the street is the prison of c. 1790. Little can be seen of Haycock's building, but the entrance porch, reputedly by Telford, is of heavily rusticated stonework decorated in a sort of pockmarked style. A square door is flanked by twin bows, each containing rectangular and circular windows. At the top is a bust of the famous prison reformer, simply marked 'Howard'.

A walk over the railway bridge and under the castle walls brings you into Castle Street. Walk up about a hundred yards on the left-hand side and turn down the narrow street called Windsor Place. Windsor House is an outstanding five-bay urban mansion. There appears to be uncertainty about its date; some authorities place it in the 1740s, others fifty years later. It certainly has the restraint of the later eighteenth century, and its door has Ionic pilasters which were then becoming popular. On the other hand it has three storeys — fairly uncommon after 1750, when two-and-a-half storeys became the norm. Was it altered late in the century?

Visible from here is the immense façade of the former Royal Salop Infirmary, designed by Edward Haycock and built in the late 1820s. As might be expected of an important public building at this time, it is ashlar-faced and Greek in character, of nine bays with the second and eighth projecting. The usual two-and-a-half storeys are supplemented by attics half-hidden in the low

As a major public building of the early nineteenth century Edward Haycock's Infirmary at Shrewsbury was inevitably built in Greek Revival style, exemplified by the heavy Doric portico. The accommodation was later supplemented by additional attic rooms.

Dignified terraced houses of c. 1840 in Whitehall Street, Shrewsbury.

roof. The dominant feature is the portico, its pediment supported by four fluted Doric columns.

Continue along Dogpole, past the Guildhall (the ancestor of all the buildings we are looking at) and down Wyle Cop. Here the hotch-potch of the Lion Hotel dominates the street, its upper section very tall with three-and-a-half storeys and five bays, with a subsidiary bay over the coach arch, where people used to await the arrival of the London mail. The lower three-storey section is also recognisably of the late eighteenth century, while the centre consists of a timber-framed building turned into the urban equivalent of a Gothick folly. This was a very smart inn indeed; apart from the fine lion over the Tuscan porch it must have resembled an elegant private house.

Across the English Bridge (c. 1770), Abbey Foregate had long been an important suburb expanding along the London road, and it duly acquired a mix of new and refaced eighteenth-century houses. In the far corner of the Abbey precinct Abbey House and Abbeydale House are neighbouring houses of the first years of the century. The former is quite ambitious in the new formal style — six bays and three storeys, quoined, parapeted and with a balustrade over its porch (the bay window is a later addition). Abbeydale House is more conservative with its steep-pitched roof and dormers in the 'Queen Anne' style.

Whitehall Street is less well-known than it should be. Halfway up is Whitehall Terrace — a delightful example of Regency elegance from the early Victorian years. The four houses are unified by their window pattern — pedimented on the outer houses, flat-headed with brackets on the inner — and by a full-length wrought-iron balcony supported on iron columns. A parapet hides the attic windows. Just beyond it there is a further surprise — a totally symmetrical terrace of eleven small villas, arranged 4-3-4 and unified by giving a single long balcony to the centre three and individual ones to the outer houses. Like Whitehall Terrace these are probably early Victorian, but they hark back very authentically to the Regency.

After returning over the river, turn left at the bottom of Wyle Cop into St Julians Friars. At the far end on the river bank is the Stone House, a riverside villa with a porch of paired Doric columns. The street side is fairly bland, but the river front is more adventurous, having an elaborate porch with fluted columns and bow windows on the ground floor, as well as pilasters and an eaves cornice.

From Wyle Cop walk into the High Street and almost immediately up Fish Street on the right. The churches of St Julian and St Alkmund stand close together, both examples of eighteenth-century renovation by T. F. Pritchard and Carline and Tilley respectively. Their conservative Gothic styles are of no great interest architecturally, but the interior of St Alkmund's is a striking example of a unified chancel and nave. A single unobtrusive arch demarcates the sanctuary, and the sense of space is emphasised by a very wide roof with no intermediate support. Francis Egerton's bold east window of 1795 is justly famous.

A short cut through Grope Lane brings you to the Square. The new shops on the left-hand side replaced an 1830s Shire Hall by Robert Smirke, and the dominant building now is the late sixteenth-century Market Hall. It masks the imposing façade of the Music Hall, which was built in about 1839 by Edward Haycock. It has much in common with his Infirmary; no doubt because of the confined space, the portico — four Ionic columns supporting a pediment — is attached, and embellishes the first floor only, leaving an unobstructed entrance below. Note the sequence of pedimented and straight-headed windows on the first floor.

Turn left in front of the Music Hall and continue up Princess Street, which has some good examples of the sort of new buildings and refacings that transformed the appearance of the town centre in the early eighteenth century. At the end Belmont leads away uphill, and we enter an area of notable Georgian and early nineteenth-century development.

The Liberal Club, at the bottom of Belmont, is the most spectacular example in Shrewsbury of a brick-cased timber-framed building. The front, of seven bays and three storeys, is restrained in the late-Georgian manner, with a Grecian touch provided by the rusticated door surround. Like other houses in the street the more impressive façade is on the river side, and from Town Walls it is possible to see the real height of the building and its projecting bays on each side. Prominent on the other side of the churchyard is 1 College Hill, formerly a bank and built in the early nineteenth century in the usual dignified Grecian manner — a severe rectangle with a heavy eaves cornice, a stuccoed ground floor and first-floor windows flanked by pilasters.

Nos. 5 and 6 Belmont were noted in the previous volume as early essays in the classical mode, and their homeliness compares interestingly with Nos. 11-13, built nearly a hundred years later. This twelve-bay structure has the centre four bays projecting, but the three doors do not conform to the symmetry. The fanlights were an innovation at the turn of the eighteenth century, and the broken pediments surmounting them are a fairly rare feature in the town. No. 15 is probably contemporary with its neighbours, but has an unusual projecting centre bay with side windows. The very elaborate rusticated door surround has an enriched window above and an attic window set uncomfortably at the top. The garden front (visible from Town Walls) is equally unusual, with a Venetian doorway and window and storeyed bay windows.

Opposite the junction of Belmont and Town Walls is The Crescent. This attempt of c. 1800 to emulate the famous Regency spas does not impress on the street side, and once again it is necessary to study the river frontage to see the full height and elaboration of the four houses. The street façade does, however, reveal a novel fashion note with its blind arches and bat-wing fanlights over the doors. The notable terrace opposite (Crescent Place) is probably the most sophisticated in the town; it dates from about 1840 and the design has a conscious elegance with its sequence of porches, windows and blind arches on the stuccoed ground floor. The huge first-floor windows must have been a striking modern feature at the time.

The next point of interest lies a few yards along Town Walls opposite the medieval guard tower, where the gates forming the main entrance to Swan Hill Court House allow a glimpse of the grounds and the house beyond. It was originally the town residence of the Marquess of Bath and dates from 1761, hence the very generous grounds in an area where building space was to be at a premium a few years later. It is the only example in Shrewsbury of eighteenth-century *rus in urbe*, a country house planted in a town. The house itself is apparently by T. F. Pritchard and has a five-bay centre with lower wings. The three-bay pediment is embellished with swags and a coat of arms.

Almost opposite the gates is the former Ebenezer Chapel of 1834, severely classical and very characteristic of its time. The five-bay façade has tall, round-headed windows, the centre one tripartite. They are flanked by pilasters. The twin projecting porches have fluted Doric columns, and the eaves cornice and pediment are dentillated. A little further along on the right is another early nineteenth-century building by Edward Haycock. Originally Allatt's School, it is a distinctive design comprising a central two-storey block

The garden front of 15 Belmont, Shrewsbury, reveals an ambitious structure of twin projecting wings with a variety of window designs. As at the nearby Liberal Club, the scale of the building is not evident on the street side.

Swan Hill Court House, Shrewsbury, was built in the mid-eighteenth century when space was plentiful, so it has the atmosphere of a country house.

with two doors; passages with round-arched windows lead to one-storey flanking wings. Very plain and ashlar-faced, it is a further example of Haycock's austere Greek style.

The view is now dominated by St Chad's church, the masterpiece of George Steuart. It was built in the early 1790s to replace the collapsed church of St Chad, and represents an innovative design that remained controversial for the next hundred years. The nave is a low rotunda where tall, round-headed gallery windows alternate with pairs of Ionic pilasters. An elliptical ante-room separates the nave from the high tower, which is in three sections — a plain square structure supporting an octagonal tower with louvred openings and paired pilasters, and finally a dome supported on eight Corinthian columns. The entrance façade has a portico of four Tuscan columns and a pediment. The interior is equally striking. The tower provides a spacious entrance hall, while the ante-room contains the light and elegant twin staircases to the gallery. The rotunda accommodates nave and chancel in one, the sanctuary being marked off by big paired columns on each side and a further sequence of columns at the back. The east window is Venetian in design. A double row of slender cast-iron columns support the gallery, from which further columns extend to the ceiling.

Just beyond the church, at the top of Claremont Bank, is the fourteen-bay terrace designed by Carline and Tilley and known as Claremont Buildings. Of early nineteenth-century date, it is a solid Grecian composition with the usual rusticated ground floor and two projecting entrances asymmetrically placed. The former St Chad's vicarage on a knoll opposite had its Georgian façade embellished by a prominent bow in the early nineteenth century.

Walk back past the church to Quarry Place, which extends down towards the river. There are some distinguished terraced houses of the late eighteenth century here, featuring the bat-wing fanlights adopted in The Crescent. The outstanding house is No. 6, a five-bay structure with round-headed windows set in arches and a fine doorway with attached Corinthian columns and an enriched window above. Before leaving the riverside there is a chance to look across at T. F. Pritchard's Foundling Hospital of 1765, now part of Shrewsbury School. The original severe thirteen-bay front was embellished with window pediments and an elaborate door surround in the 1880s.

From the top of Quarry Place there is a view into St John's Hill, where Nos. 19-26 provide an excellent example of harmonious terracing incorporating quite distinct individual styles. The unifying feature is a dentillated eaves cornice of uniform height. One house here has an unusual wide, round-headed door with a huge keystone, while another has doors given a Venetian appearance by the addition of small side windows. They all have cellars, but with no street access. Further down St John's Hill, Hardwick House (No. 12) was possibly the first classical house to appear in this fashionable suburb. Built soon after 1700, its Baroque features, including giant pilasters, heavy cornice below the attics and Flemish gables on its wings, are an instructive contrast to the more restrained façades of the later eighteenth century.

Two other structures should be mentioned. To the north of the town centre, off the A49 in Spring Gardens is a former flax mill, later used as a maltings and believed to be the world's first iron-framed building. It was built c. 1797 from castings made in William Hazeldine's Shrewsbury factory. At the eastern end of Abbey Foregate outside the Shirehall, the Greek Doric column bearing a statue of Lord Hill was erected in 1816. At over 130 feet high it is a considerable achievement.

Wem

One would not expect to find classic Georgian architecture in a small town like Wem, but some interesting survivals from the period are there to be sought out.

Starting at the eastern end of the High Street, at the entrance to the main car park, one notices at once the cheerful frontage of the Castle Inn — three storeys with large sash windows (those on the attic storey unusually horizontal) and a columned porch. Further down on the left is the town's most impressive Georgian house, now the National Westminster Bank. It scorns the eighteenth-century obsession with symmetry by having six bays, and its off-set 'centre' is emphasised by an enriched window case over the doorway. Otherwise the façade is plain with just an eaves cornice and string course.

The old Market Hall next to the church is obviously of the early nineteenth century, but retains favourite Georgian features such as the twelve-light sash windows, the eaves cornice and prominent quoins. Next door No. 67 appears to be of the very early nineteenth century with its smart ashlar-faced façade and two-and-a-half storey design. Round the bend in the road Astley House is claimed to be of c. 1740. If so, it was built in very old-fashioned style with flush windows and crude lintels. Next to it is an example of faded elegance — No. 91 is a most distinctive house with a double bow front (the bows of unequal sizes) and a porch embellished with ironwork. This is usually characteristic of Regency style, and it is unusual to find such a building in an unfashionable country town. Let us hope it does not decay much further.

Some of the most attractive of Wem's buildings are to be found in the side streets. Noble Street contains some good early nineteenth-century cottages as well as the Conservative Club, a mid-Georgian house with hipped roof, a central eaves pediment in the cornice and segment-headed windows (possibly

An unusual house in Wem, with a double bow front and decorative ironwork that give it an appearance of a kind associated with the Regency period. It is possibly an adaptation of an earlier and smaller building.

added later). The chapel in Chapel Street is of 1834, ashlar-faced and with a columned porch, an interesting contrast with later, more fanciful, Victorian chapels. Chapel Street also contains Benedict House, of two-and-a-half storeys and with the restrained façade typical of the later eighteenth century, and a pleasant trio of attached houses that probably have timber frames behind their Georgian façades. Note the unusual round-headed lights in the windows of No. 24.

Finally, Wem has three excellent examples of the sort of house built by Georgian professional men who wished to move to more secluded areas of the town without the inconvenience of a long ride to work. In Mill Lane is Roden House, very severe and dignified with a Greek-style porch. It dates from the early years of the nineteenth century. The fine house in New Street opposite the garage is older but a classic late-Georgian design — three bays, elaborate projecting porch, hipped roof and enriched centre window on the first floor. A solid house for a solid citizen. Of similar character is the house on the extreme edge of the town beside the road to Ellesmere, although this one appears to retain much of its original stabling.

Whitchurch

The town centre of Whitchurch did not undergo drastic changes in the Georgian period. One or two brand new buildings appeared, and there was the usual refacing of older structures, but most of the Georgian development was concentrated in new 'suburbs'.

Surprisingly the church of 1712 did not become a focal point for fashionable residences. The only characteristic buildings of the period in the immediate vicinity are the row of early nineteenth-century artisans' cottages in Yardington and the Higginson almshouses. The cottages have inevitably been altered by the addition of new doors and windows, but one original sliding window survives in the second house down. The almshouses were rebuilt at the turn of the eighteenth century with a very low-pitched roof decorated with eaves modillions, and with a façade unified by a heavily-quoined central bay containing a niche. The drip mouldings over the doors are a throwback to the Stuart period.

The High Street reveals a good deal of refacing and remodelling, an obvious example being the Victoria Hotel, an old coaching inn given big new sash windows and a smart porch with Ionic columns in the Greek style. Several other buildings in the street date from the earlier eighteenth century period discussed in Volume 2.

At the bottom of the High Street Green End leads away to the left. The only Georgian buildings of real interest are at the far end where Talbot House and Weston House present an interesting comparison. Talbot House is an early and naive attempt at 'classical' style, with its flush windows, thick glazing bars and three string courses decorated by crude modillions. Weston House is probably not much later, but it shows greater refinement and restraint — the single string course, moulded window frames and finely-made doorcase with Corinthian pilasters give it some claim to elegance.

The other notable Georgian structures are in Dodington. Close to the corner of Bark Hill is an unusual pair of semi-detached houses, each of four bays and the fashionable two-and-a-half-storey arrangement — a very restrained façade with just a plain string course beneath the attic storey. Further up we have the sad sight of the former Mansion House converted to a supermarket, its ground floor ruined and its upper storeys neglected. Enough remains to hint at a most impressive façade — five bays, three storeys, roof parapet, eaves cornice with modillions, keystoned lintels and the characteristic Georgian feature of an enriched surround for the window over the main entrance. The pedimented front door with console brackets survives.

Next comes St Catherine's Church of 1836, deconsecrated but deserving much better than to be left in shabby disuse. Its Greek style is unique in Shropshire. The ashlar-faced front is dominated by the impressive entrance featuring attached Ionic columns and the low tower made up of an octagon of pillars. The almshouses opposite date from 1829, but were built in an early seventeenth-century style with symmetrical gables and drip mouldings. On the other side of Bridgewater Street is the unusual sight of two three-bay houses given a kind of unity by having their eaves pediments placed side by side.

Finally, at the corner of Rosemary Lane, is the smartest Georgian house in the town. Cherwell House is of very plain brick with an invisible roof and a pedimented eaves cornice. The three wide bays suggest a spacious interior, and the big windows decrease in size through the three storeys. The restrained effect is completed by a simple porch with console brackets.

Part Six
Looking at Buildings: The Countryside

(Unless it is specifically stated, the houses listed in the gazetteer are NOT open to the public. Where a building can be seen from a public road or path the map reference is followed by an asterisk*. Map references are preceded by the OS sheet number.)

Acton Burnell

126: 532021 *. The outstanding building of the period here is the Hall (now Concord College) visible from the Kenley road. The exterior was remodelled in the early years of the nineteenth century to provide a façade in the Greek Revival style, with a giant portico of massive Ionic columns supporting a pediment — a little pretentious for a fairly modest house. The north-eastern side features symmetrical canted bay windows.

Apley Park

138: 715985. The writer was unable to view Apley Park personally, but it is recorded as a Gothick mansion of 1811 in Grinshill stone.

Ashford Bowdler

Ashford Hall (137: 514712 *) is best viewed from the main road, where its façade makes an impressive sight. Dating from the mid-eighteenth century, it is an example of a substantial country house of the period when the Baroque showiness of 1700-1730 was giving way to Georgian restraint. Nevertheless it retains the big three-bay eaves pediment typical of the earlier fashion. The outbuildings include a stable block with cupola.

In the small hamlet (137: 517706 *) is a splendid late-Georgian farmhouse (best viewed from the main road lay-by). Its sophisticated façade includes a fanlighted door and two Venetian windows on the ground floor. A large brick barn of the period stands nearby. On the other side of the lane is another large but less ambitious farmhouse.

Asterley (Pontesbury)

126: 374073 *. The Methodist chapel here is dated 1834 and is a tiny rectangular building. Its large round-headed windows, with iron glazing bars forming an attractive design, are identical to those in the chapels at Pontesbury and Minsterley, and were probably purpose-built in large quantities during this prolific period of chapel building.

Aston Hall (Oswestry)

126: 326274. Built by James Wyatt in the 1780s, Aston Hall reflects the trend at this time towards neo-classical austerity. It is a restrained house of seven

The Methodist chapel at Asterley, near Pontesbury. Many tiny country chapels were built in this simple style in the 1830s. They can usually be identified by their tall, round-headed windows.

bays and two storeys, faced with fine grey ashlar stone. There is no portico — the single-storey porch is flanked by pilasters and attached Ionic columns. Otherwise the main embellishments are niches and carved garlands at the corners.

The detached chapel dates from the 1740s and is built of the customary brick with stone dressings.

Atcham

Hardly noticed by drivers on the busy A5, Atcham is full of interest for the architectural enthusiast. The dominant building is the Mytton and Mermaid Hotel (126: 542093 *), a splendid house in the restrained later Georgian manner. Of seven bays and two-and-a-half storeys, it retains the hipped roof popular in the early years of the eighteenth century, but apart from the pedimented doorway the only embellishment is on the river frontage, where bow windows extend the full height of the house. The elegant stable block looks like a slightly later addition.

Next to the filling station, and easily missed, is a thatched 'cottage ornée' with Gothick windows — actually a semi-detached pair, and no doubt built as fanciful estate housing. The theme is repeated in the adjacent L-shaped row of cottages; they have been heavily renovated, but the Gothick windows survive around the corner. Another Gothick survival, the western gate lodge

This is part of a range of estate cottages which have been modernised. The striking ogee-headed window projection is a reminder of their original Gothick character.

of the Attingham estate, stands half a mile up the Upton Magna road (126: 542100).

Luckily, John Gwynne's fine bridge of 1771 (126: 540093 *) was left in position when the present bridge was constructed in 1929. It carried Telford's Holyhead Road, and one of the original milestones can be seen on the western side. It is well worth getting down on to the river bank to see the details of the bridge, which is quite steeply pitched with six water arches, each with rusticated voussoirs and a vermiculated keystone.

The old Atcham bridge, designed by John Gwynne in about 1770, once carried the Holyhead road. It was replaced in 1929.

Attingham Park

126: 550099. **National Trust. Open to the public.** The original building here was a small Queen Anne house of 1701. In 1783 Noel Hill, first Lord Berwick, commissioned George Steuart, a little-known Scottish architect, to build a mansion incorporating the earlier house, Steuart produced a design in the austere neo-classical taste of the time — a sort of refined Palladianism. A new eleven-bay central block was built in front of the old house, and colonnaded passages connected it to service wings on each side. The material is Grinshill ashlar stone. The main house is unusually tall, and its façade is dominated by a giant portico with four slender Ionic columns. The second Lord Berwick commissioned John Nash to add a gallery to house his extensive collection of pictures, and this room of 1802 is of great interest as an early experiment with iron and glass.

Brogyntyn (Oswestry)

126: 279312 *. Brogyntyn Hall was originally built in the 1730s as a replacement for an older house. At that date it would have been of red brick with stone dressings in the provincial Baroque style, and thus it remained until it was drastically modernised in about 1810. The chosen style was vaguely Grecian in the fashion which had been established a few years earlier at Longford Hall (Newport) and continued at Willey Park and Coton Hall. The brick was rendered, most of the embellishments removed and a giant Ionic portico constructed on the entrance front. The east side was later extended.

Broseley

Broseley, one of those indeterminate places that is neither village nor town, is predominantly Victorian, but among the later infill there are still plentiful examples of artisans' housing from the late eighteenth and early nineteenth centuries.

The older settlement straggles beside a long main road that starts as Church Street in the east, becomes the High Street and ends as Barratt's Hill. The two notable large houses of the period are close to the church. Broseley Hall (127: 678015 *) is a conventional mansion of the mid-eighteenth century with a segmental pediment over the door, while the Lawns (**Open to the public**) is an interesting mixture of styles — the quoins and the tall, segment-headed windows are typical of its original early date (1727), but the large bow at the front is an alteration reflecting the Regency fashion of the 1800s.

Little of interest remains in the High Street, apart from No. 29, of two-and-a-half storeys and with prominent canted bays, and No. 17, which has four big tripartite windows and a centre first-floor window with a pattern of glazing bars. Both appear to be of the early nineteenth century. On Barratt's Hill is a range of medium-sized houses of the same period, and others are visible across the valley. A little way down the hill on the right is Tanglewood, a twin-gabled cottage dated 1742, and the smartened-up house above it is in the same style.

At the end of Chapel Lane, off the top of the High Street, is the Baptist chapel of 1742 (127: 671018 *), an unassuming brick building with tall, round-headed windows. The manse is a later addition.

Caynton Hall (Ryton)

127: 778029 *. A very elegant country house, immediately recognisable as of Regency date. Built of stuccoed brick, the entrance front has seven bays, the centre three forming a shallow bow with a miniature Tuscan portico at ground-floor level. Passages connect to low wings on each side.

Caynton House (Newport)

127: 705218 *. This is a magnificent example of an eighteenth-century gentleman farmer's residence, and is still used as a farmhouse. It is of two-and-a-half storeys and has a five-bay centre with lower one-bay wings. The main embellishments are a heavy eaves cornice and a wide entrance door with Ionic pilasters and a segmental fanlight. The window arches are of plain brick. The house stands close to some fine barns and stabling of the period.

Cleobury Mortimer

The main street has a fine array of Georgian cased timber-framing but few outstanding individual buildings. At the western end of the village (138: 668756 *) is a terrace of four well-preserved artisans' cottages of the early nineteenth century. Further east on the right (138: 673757 *) the Manor House is one of the best Queen Anne houses in the county — built well before the start of this period, of course, but a reminder that not everyone in those early years chose ostentatious provincial Baroque. The Vicarage, in the main street opposite the church, is a fine example of timber-framing cased in local stone. At the east end of the town, opposite the Post Office, are two interesting early nineteenth-century houses; they were obviously identical originally, but one had unmatched bow windows added to the ground floor. A path opposite the Vicarage leads up to the Lacon Childe School, which has an attractive building of 1740 — basically Queen Anne even at this date, with five bays, a neat doorcase, a hipped roof with dormers and a tall cupola.

Clun

This is a very Georgian town, although its character derives from small and irregular façades. The distinctive building of the period is the Court House (137: 300809 *), a well-proportioned market building of three bays and one-and-a-half storeys with a hipped roof and cupola. The doors and windows are plain stone arches (originally open), and there is a semi-circular window on the first floor. It was built in the 1780s but looks much earlier. Nearby, on the road down to the bridge, is Cresswell House, difficult to date but probably very late eighteenth century — three broad bays, with the centre projecting and topped with a gable pediment containing a semi-circular window like that at the Court House.

Coalbrookdale — *See* Part Three.

This farmhouse at Shotatton illustrates the changing social status of the more prosperous farmers in the late eighteeth century. The occupant would probably have moved from a timber-framed house in a nearby village.

Built in 1742 of coursed limestone, Linley Hall has the precise proportions and restrained character of the true Palladian style. This austere fashion was to be revived nearly a hundred years later.

Hawkstone Hall. The central block was a provincial Baroque house of the 1720s with the usual stone dressings, giant pilasters and pedimented central bays. In the mid-eighteenth century substantial wings were added to each side and given curious apse-like ends.

The Citadel, Hawkstone Park — an early example (1790s) of the restrained taste for the Picturesque which was later to appear in more exaggerated forms in houses such as Quatford Castle.

Woodhouse near Rednal.

When the versatile John Nash rebuilt Longner Hall in 1803 he produced a design that grafted a glazed Gothic arcade on to a house reminiscent of an Elizabethan mansion. The result was as original as his other Shropshire house, Cronkhill.

Cresswell House, Clun, is an attempt to combine the usual Georgian two-and-a-half storey arrangement with a traditional pitched roof. As a result the eaves pediment encloses a dormer window.

Condover

A short distance to the west of the church gate (126: 494057 *) is a rare example of a Georgian semi-detached house in the countryside. It is dated 1777 and has three bays; the twin front doors are set side by side under a single pediment, and the illusion of a single house is furthered by means of a false central window over the doors.

Coton Hall

138: 774864. Dating from the early years of the nineteenth century, Coton represents the austere style at the opposite end of the spectrum from the Regency prettiness of the same period. Faced with grey ashlar, it has seven bays and two storeys (the low attic storey universally popular throughout the later eighteenth century disappeared from many houses built at this time.) There is a simple porch supported by pairs of columns, and the windows are completely plain with thin glazing bars. The symmetry and simplicity of the house were impaired by a florid extra wing added by a Victorian owner.

Cronkhill

126: 536083 *. This unique house by John Nash has the distinction of being the earliest known Regency villa in the Italian style. It originally formed part of the Attingham estate, and in the tradition of fanciful estate building it is completely irregular in design, comprising a square block with two towers, one round and one square, attached. The front of the house is given unity by an L-shaped colonnade with a balustrade that forms a first-floor balcony. It is a building of great charm.

Coton Hall, near Alveley, is a typical small country house of the early nineteenth century, when stone had come back in favour. A portico would have been inappropriate for a house of this size, but it has a very emphatic four-columned porch. The wing on the left is Victorian.

Decker Hill (Shifnal Golf Club)

127: 752096. This is a smart Regency house with a low elevation (the roof is almost flat) and a façade of tall, elegant windows on the side confronting the visitor. The entrance porch is tucked away on the north side and has a wide, recessed porch with a big segmental fanlight, flanked by giant Ionic columns. The very thin glazing bars are typical of the Regency period.

Diddlebury

137: 510852. Delbury Hall (c. 1750) has been referred to in the introduction as exemplifying the new taste for dignified plainness. It consists of a central block of seven bays and two-and-a-half storeys, with flanking two-storey wings. The severity of the façade is relieved only by dentillated brickwork beneath the eaves. The original front door was adapted in the early nineteenth century to provide the fanlight arrangement popular at the time. An elegant stable block and handsome barn stand nearby.

We can also see here an early interest in the possibilities of landscaping. Although the house stands close to the village, the main drive is designed to involve the longest possible journey through the park, and the house remains invisible until the last moment, when it is dramatically revealed at the bottom of a slope.

Dudleston

126: 347377. Half a mile south of the village, Plas Iolyn is a substantial house of the early 1800s, with an expensive ashlar front but rather more economical brick at the rear, which is twin-gabled in a fashion reminiscent of the seventeenth century. The house is unusually designed with the two outer bays of its façade lower than the centre.

Edgmond

Edgmond Hall, almost opposite the church entrance (127: 721192), is an interesting small country house of the late eighteenth century. The three-bay centre is flanked by lower one-bay wings, and the house still retains the hipped roof fashionable fifty years before. The square porch has a neat pedimented door with fluted pilasters. The big bay windows which hug the porch closely are no doubt nineteenth-century additions. The house is currently used as a residential centre by Sandwell Education Authority.

Felhampton

137: 445873 *. Beside the A49 about three miles north of Craven Arms, Felhampton Court exemplifies the minor country house built from a pattern book. It no doubt dates from the mid-eighteenth century and is fashionably plain, but it conforms to no architectural rules. The dominant feature is an immense eaves pediment containing a window, which, if genuine, lights a garret above the attic rooms. The first floor has a central Venetian window (a favourite Palladian feature), and immediately above is a semi-circular window, another Palladian whim.

Ford

Ford House and the Mansion House, situated on either side of the church (126: 414138 *), illustrate vividly the changing architectural tastes of the eighteenth century. Ford House has the showy features typical of the early years of the century — a Tuscan porch, steep pitched roof with dormers, pilastered doorway, decorated eaves cornice, prominent quoins and big chimney stacks. The Mansion House, built in 1779 and oddly urban-looking, has a very plain façade. The only embellished window is over the entrance, and the cornice is undecorated. The centre three bays project slightly and have a brick eaves pediment bearing a dignified garland design. There is no real porch, but the entrance is flanked by attached columns.

Frodesley

The church (126: 516011 *) dates from 1809. It is built in rubble masonry with angle pilasters in ashlar and a small timber-framed belfry, and the general effect was no doubt intended to be medieval. The Victorian north aisle in conventional ashlar masonry looks distinctly out of place. The interior shows a striking contrast between chancel and nave. The oak-panelled sanctuary includes a reredos with characteristic pilasters, while the east window is contained in a finely-crafted wooden case. The whole effect is unexpectedly rich when compared to the homely box pews and general plainness of the nave. The church deserves to be better known.

Great Ness

For some reason, the tiny village of Great Ness has more than the usual share of large houses of the period. Great Ness Hall (126: 396189 *) has the full-height canted bays that seem to have become popular in the county at the end of the eighteenth century (they are exactly similar to those on the river frontage of the Liberal Club in Belmont, Shrewsbury). Opposite is Great Ness House (126: 396187 *), rather earlier and with a double pitched roof, while at the lane junction to the west (126: 397188 *) is an excellent example of the kind of smaller Georgian villa for a superior middle-class family.

Nearby: Between Kinton and Wilcott, on the other side of the A5 (126: 374194 *), is the tiny Wilcott Congregational chapel of 1834, a plain rectangle built of sandstone rubble.

Hatton Grange

127: 766044. This is not an exciting house, but is of some importance as being one of the few country mansions in Shropshire built between 1740 and 1760. Dating from 1748, it obviously retains some of the provincial Baroque influences of twenty years before, especially in the decorated eaves pediment, but it also demonstrates the new taste for greater simplicity of detail, and the canted bay windows are an innovation.

Haughton Hall

127: 743084. Of seven bays and two storeys, the main house is dated 1718 and is fairly typical of the time with its attic dormers partially concealed behind an eaves parapet and its impressive show of chimneys. The fashion of a hundred years later produced the little one-bay flanking 'pavilions' with pyramid roofs, connected to the house by passageways columned to resemble porches.

Hawkstone Hall

126: 583301. The Hall is brick-built and consists of a central block connected to flanking wings by curved two-storey passages. The two-and-a-half storey centre section is the original house, completed in 1722. It has nine bays, the outer ones taking the form of square towers, strongly emphasised by quoins and having their own pyramid roofs. The entrance occupies the centre three bays, which are stuccoed and embellished with four giant Corinthian columns supporting a substantial frieze. (This feature seems too sophisticated for the 1720s and may well have been added when the wings were built.) The three-bay centre is surmounted by an eaves pediment, and a cornice runs the full width of the building below the attic storey. The pavilions are of five bays and two storeys and date from the middle of the eighteenth century. They feature giant pilasters which continue round the unusual semi-circular ends. Symmetry in the wings is deliberately avoided by placing the entrance doors off-centre.

The house is a religious college, and in recent years a church and a residential block have been added.

Hawkstone was famous in its time for the extravagance of its park, which reflected rather melodramatically the taste for the Picturesque in the later eighteenth century. Devised by Sir Rowland Hill and his son Richard, the grounds included a ruined castle, an Awful Precipice, a zoo and a hermitage with hermit. The landscapers were able to take advantage of the natural sandstone crags which occur here. Most of the features still exist, but are now in the ownership of the Hawkstone Park Hotel, and the park can only be visited with permission.

The entrance lodge, usually in a whimsical design chosen by the house owner, became a familiar sight from the mid-eighteenth century onwards. This example is at Hopton Wafers.

Nearby: 126: 571285 *. Just off the road between Weston and Marchamley is The Citadel, built as a dower house in the 1790s and an early example of the castle style that became so popular during the Regency. It is of red sandstone with three castellated towers.

Hopton Wafers

The church here (138: 637765 *) dates from 1827, a neat structure in ashlar stone, but there is a touch of Regency frivolity in the strange saw-edge castellation. Later Victorian windows have given the church a Gothic look, but the original windows would have been the tall, round-headed type characteristic of the early nineteenth century. Immediately opposite is Hopton Manor (138: 638765 *), a very tall late Georgian house with an odd feature — there are the usual three bays, but the eaves pediment over the centre is set to one side as though the building has been stretched. The canted bay windows may well be a later addition. At the back is a stable block and a row of attached cottages. A short distance to the north-east (138: 642766 *) is Hopton Court, a big Georgian house, rather featureless apart from a colonnade supporting a balcony, added in the early 1800s. The house has a fine position and is best viewed from the main road just west of the village.

Ironbridge — *See* Part Three.

Jackfield

127: 687030 *. This was a centre of Victorian prosperity, based on the manufacture of encaustic tiles. The earlier buildings were beside the river, and below St Mary's church a row of them still stand. They appear to be of the early eighteenth century, but may be brick casings of older houses. One of them has dormers set in the eaves, a style that appears elsewhere in the Severn Gorge, for example at Teakettle Row in Coalbrookdale.

Linley Hall

137: 344930. This is the only Palladian house in Shropshire to have been built when the fashion was at its height in the first half of the eighteenth century.

It dates from the 1740s and the architect was Henry Joynes, who had been an associate of the celebrated Baroque architect Sir John Vanbrugh. Built in compact cubic form of limestone cut to the size and shape of bricks, the house has many typical Palladian features in miniature. The bottom storey is a service basement faced with deeply-rusticated ashlar stone on the entrance front (the purpose of this was to give an impression of rough strength at the base of the structure.) The entrance door also follows the curious Palladian fashion of being set in the basement, from which an interior staircase gives access to the piano nobile or ground floor, which is several feet above ground level. It is distinguished on the entrance front by a fine enriched Venetian window.

The five-bay main façade is on the south side, where the outer bays project and are surmounted by modillioned pediments. There is direct access to the piano nobile here by means of steps and an Ionic porch. The west side is dominated by a full-height canted bay.

Close to the house is a magnificent stable block of rubble limestone with its own elaborate nine-bay façade, featuring a central door with a Gibbs surround and a modillioned pediment over the centre three bays.

Longford (Newport)

127: 728183. Longford Hall (now a school) was built in the 1790s to a design by Joseph Bonomi, a former assistant to Robert Adam. In his later years Bonomi became an enthusiast for the Greek Revival, and the Hall has a consequent dignity and severity. Of ashlar construction, the house is of seven bays and two storeys, producing a low configuration. The façade is dominated by a massive portico supported on four bulbous Tuscan columns, and the principal decoration is a deep eaves cornice continued round the portico. Unobtrusive pilasters mark the angles and flank the centre bay. An individual note is struck by the big semi-circular window over the door.

On the other side of the road past the Hall (127: 726185 *), the roofless church of St Mary stands forlornly with its walls bulging. Built in about 1805, it is a compact rectangular structure with a small tower and an apse to accommodate the sanctuary. In the fashion of the day the tower and nave are castellated.

Longner Hall

126: 528111. Not to be confused with Longnor Hall near Dorrington. The architect for Longner, reconstructed in 1803, was John Nash, who also built the Italianate villa at Cronkhill. Here he produced a design that was distinctly Elizabethan in character, with the use of red sandstone and grey stone dressings, but Longner has one feature in common with Cronkhill — an L-shaped colonnade on the garden front. It is glazed like a conservatory, with mock-medieval windows, and has a castellated top. The gable-end bay windows on this side and on the south-eastern front are enriched with elaborate wooden window cases. There are extensive stables and outbuildings.

The Lyth (Ellesmere)

126: 410335. This is a most intriguing house dating from 1819. It is built in plain brick to a severely rectangular plan, but any austerity is banished by the tall verandah of patterned cast iron that surrounds it. The entrance front faces east and is literally a façade — the windows are glazed but blind. By contrast the garden front, facing south, has huge ground-floor windows. It is a house designed for someone who wanted sunshine, and indeed the first owner was apparently a West Indies plantation owner. What he built was an example of 'colonial Regency', a fair imitation of the traditional plantation mansion.

Madeley

127: 696041 *. The church (1796) was designed by Thomas Telford in a characteristic classical style (cf. St Mary's, Bridgnorth). The nave is octagonal on the outside and faced with large ashlar blocks (the 'apse' at the east end is a much later addition.) The pairs of iron-framed windows are round-headed on the gallery level and rectangular below. The short, square tower ascends from a base that forms a pedimented entrance façade.

Maesbury Marsh

126: 314250. This is a former canal centre, and the Navigation Inn is the only survivor of several inns on the Llanymynech branch of the Ellesmere Canal. Along the Oswestry road Sycamore House has the bow-front typical of the canal company's more palatial houses, and a little further on is a short terrace of tiny eighteenth-century labourers' cottages. Other terraces of this type in the village have now been spoilt by tasteless modernisation.

The turnpike tollhouse at Minsterley shows that the taste for quaint Gothick continued well into the nineteenth century.

Millichope Park

138: 529884. The house was designed by Edward Haycock and completed in 1840. It is in Haycock's favourite Greek style, but much of its effect has been lost as a result of recent changes. It now appears to be built on a terrace, but the original plan was similar to that of the Music Hall in Shrewsbury — a modest entrance on the ground floor, with a massive Ionic portico beginning on the first floor. The entrance has now been removed, and the house appears quite small while retaining its elegance.

As a result of some skilful park landscaping the incoming visitor sees the best view of the house just before arrival — it stands high above a lake, with a domed temple carefully included in the prospect.

Minsterley

The turnpike toll house (126: 373051 *) is an idiosyncratic piece of Picturesque design from the early nineteenth century. It has three bays, with fanciful ogee-headed windows on the ground floor and round-headed windows above.

Moreton Say

127: 630345 *). St Margaret's church is an interesting example of the Georgian casing of an older interior. Of red brick with stone dressings, the church is severe in style with embellishment confined to the tower, which has two string courses and obelisk finials. The windows are round-headed with keystones.

Morville Hall

138: 669940 *. **National Trust. Open by written appointment with the tenant.** This is a most unusual house — built in rubble limestone, it was originally Elizabethan, and retains the emphatic projecting wings of that period, complete with turret staircases in the angles. In the mid-eighteenth century it was remodelled and given sash windows and fashionable embellishments, including half-height pilasters on the wings and a pedimented door (the fanlight must be later). At the same time twin detached 'pavilions' with cupolas were added, quite a long way from the house and connected to it by walls. The three elements make up an impressive symmetrical frontage.

Munslow

There are two houses here that exemplify the skilful use of the local limestone, which breaks out into small pieces and thus can only be used in rubble construction. The old rectory next to the church (137: 521877 *) is an elegant small house of the late eighteenth century with an Ionic porch. Hungerford Farm, beside the B4368 just over a mile to the north-east of the village (137: 537893 *), is a most imposing grey farmhouse, very plain but featuring a Venetian window as a first-floor centrepiece.

Oakley Park

137: 490763. Not viewed personally by the author, but recorded as being of early eighteenth-century origin, remodelled by John Haycock in c. 1784, then again by C. R. Cockerell in 1819-36. (Cockerell had been to Greece, and copied several of his findings in the design.) Of red brick, the house has a screen with double Doric porticos on the entrance front and an attached portico with pilasters and balcony on the south front.

Pontesbury

The timber-framed house opposite the church gates (126: 400061 *) has been subdivided into three tiny units, and may well be a rare surviving example of a sixteenth-century yeoman's house converted for labourers' accommodation in the eighteenth century. The windows are modern, but the doorways, each with a crude wooden pediment, seem to be part of the original conversion.

Prees

126: 557335 *. Prees Hall, opposite the church, has a seven-bay centre apparently of the early eighteenth century. The unusual feature is that the centre three bays are very deeply recessed, well beyond the eaves pediment. The recess is flanked by brick pilasters. This block is connected to wings which appear to be unsymmetrical and of a later Georgian date. At the time of writing the house is empty and close inspection is not possible.

Rednal — *See* Canal Gazetteer in Part Three and *Woodhouse* below.

Rowton Castle

126: 376127 *. The scatter of modern buildings around Rowton Castle is a reminder that the site was used until a few years ago as a school, and is now a hotel. The original buildings have not been encroached on, however. They constitute a conventional early eighteenth-century house embedded in mock-medieval additions — an excellent example of the 'castle' craze of the early years of the nineteenth century. The romantic features include a battlemented gatehouse, a prominent round tower and various castellated structures.

Sibdon Carwood

137: 413833. Sibdon Carwood is an example of the craze for Gothicising at the turn of the eighteenth century. In this case, battlements have been added to a much earlier house, but in superficial and unconvincing fashion. The house itself is of limestone in coursed rubble construction and is reputed to date from the seventeenth century, but Georgian segment-headed windows have changed its earlier character.

Styche Hall

127: 645356 *. Notable as the birthplace of Robert Clive, the Hall is in an isolated position north-west of Market Drayton, and is perhaps best seen from the road between Longford and Longslow, where its white façade stands against a low wooded hill like a carefully-composed eighteenth-century print. Of seven bays and two-and-a-half storeys, it was rebuilt in 1762 by the distinguished architect Sir William Chambers, whose restrained style is evident in the almost total lack of embellishment (the porch and bay windows are of a later date).

Totterton Hall (Bishop's Castle)

137: 358876 *. Like several other large houses in the county, Totterton was modernised in the mid-eighteenth century by having a new block built in front of a smaller brick house. There are signs too of an even earlier stone portion. The entrance front is unusual in having full-height brick pilaster strips, a restrained echo of the giant stone pilasters popular at the beginning of the century. The centre bay of the five has a pediment raised above the eaves, which have brick dentillation. The four-column flat portico is similar to that of its near neighbour Walcot, and is a fairly rare feature.

Walcot (Lydbury North)

137: 347850 *. This is a very grand house in a fine situation. It was built in the early 1760s for Lord Clive, and the architect was the eminent Sir William Chambers, who was also responsible for remodelling Clive's birthplace, Styche Hall. In some ways it is an unusual design for the time — low (only two storeys) and very long (eleven bays) with a low four-columned portico at the entrance. Its hipped roof behind a balustrade, however, harks back to the early eighteenth century. There is extensive stabling and an additional gallery-like wing of the early nineteenth century, apparently a ballroom.

Wellington

Too few significant buildings of the period remain to justify an itinerary, but All Saints church (127: 651117) cannot be ignored. Dating from 1790, it was designed by George Steuart, architect of St Chad's, Shrewsbury, but is of a less imposing rectangular plan with an apse. The three-bay entrance front has the door and windows in identical moulded surrounds, each topped by a small semi-circular window and the whole façade is pedimented at eaves level. The low, two-stage tower has carved decoration. The nave has the common sequence of paired windows, round-headed for the gallery and rectangular on the ground floor, with carved motifs between them.

Apart from one or two early nineteenth-century pubs, the town architecture is fairly nondescript. In Walker Street the Raven has a most unusual frontage — four Venetian windows, the upper pair with fanciful ogee arches. The Mount in Haygate Road, again of the early nineteenth century, has a finely-proportioned central block with a pediment over the central bays and a most elaborate entrance under a cornice and parapet running the whole length of the ground floor. The porch is supported by four columns and contains a simple arched doorcase with a fanlight.

Willey Park

138: 667993. This is a house of c. 1820, built by the celebrated Lewis Wyatt in the dignified Grecian style. The nine-bay entrance front is dominated by a giant portico with four Corinthian columns. The south-west façade is embellished with a columned bow, a device used earlier by Robert Mylne at Woodhouse, near Rednal.

Woodhouse

126: 364288. Woodhouse was designed by Robert Mylne and built in about 1775 to incorporate a much earlier house. It is in red brick with a parapet concealing most of the low hipped roof, and both the east and south façades received special treatment since both are visible on the approach to the house. The east side is the entrance front, and here Mylne produced a unique recessed porch that is not quite a portico. It occupies three bays, and on each side of the modest entrance door is a pair of giant Ionic columns, one behind the other — a unique feature in Shropshire and perhaps in the country. The longer south façade has a central bowed feature, very shallow and embellished by four attached Ionic columns. Subdued Ionic pilasters are placed at the corners.

Glossary

This is not a general architectural glossary. It contains only those terms used in the text and applicable to Shropshire buildings of the period.

Apse: A semi-circular extension to a church, often accommodating the sanctuary or a chapel behind it.

Arcade: A series of arches carried on columns.

Ashlar: Smooth-faced building stone cut to precise right angles. Used in very high-quality building work either as structural stone or as a facing for inferior material.

Attic: The top storey of a house, usually lower in height than the others.

Baluster: One of the vertical posts, often shaped, supporting the top rail of a **balustrade**.

Balustrade: A parapet of wood or stone comprising vertical posts supporting a rail.

Bargeboards: Decorative boards fixed to the gables of a house to conceal structural timbers. Very often a Victorian addition to an earlier house.

Baroque: A style of architecture developed after 1660 by Wren and others in which the classical idiom introduced earlier by Inigo Jones was elaborated into a florid and highly individual form involving the lavish use of embellishment. It reached the remoter parts of the country in a naive form known as 'provincial Baroque'.

Bay: A term used to describe the arrangement and extent of a house façade. Any features spaced regularly along the façade can count as bays, but it is usual to apply the term to the first-floor windows. Thus a five-bay house will normally have a row of five windows on the first floor. The entrance door counts as a bay if there is no window over it.

Bay window: A projecting window on the ground floor. If the projection includes windows above it is known as a storeyed bay window. A projecting window on an upper floor only is an **oriel window.** A bay window with a regular curve is called a **bow window**.

Bond: A method of laying bricks (see Part Four).

Bow window: see **Bay window**.

Bracket: A decorative feature attached to a wall and supporting (or appearing to support) a porch, cornice etc. A console bracket has a long S-shaped profile.

Canted bay window: A bay window in the form of a half-hexagon or half-octagon.

Cased: A term used of a timber-framed house which has received an outer 'skin' of stone or brick.

Castellation: The design or adaptation of a house with the aim of making it look like a castle, especially by the addition of battlements.

Colonnade: A line of columns.

Cornice: A projecting decorative moulding running horizontally across a façade, often at the eaves but sometimes beneath the attic windows.

Dentillation: A form of decoration achieved by allowing every other brick header in a course to project, producing an effect like teeth. Normally used under eaves or as a **string course**.

Diaper work: A form of decoration usually found on walls, roofs or chimneys, consisting of a repeated pattern of diamond shapes (an effect often obtained by using bricks of different colours).

Dormer: A projecting window in a roof, designed to light the roof space and having its own miniature roof structure.

Eaves: The overhanging edge of a roof, often emphasised in classical architecture by the addition of a **cornice**.

Fanlight: A semi-circular window over an entrance door, designed to light the hall.

Finial: An embellishment, often in the form of a spike or ball, placed at the top of a gable or roof feature (usually Victorian).

Fluting: A pattern of vertical grooves in a column or **pilaster**.

Garret: A room formed within the roof of a building.

Gibbs surround: A form of door surround consisting of spaced stone blocks set vertically on each side of the door and bridged by an arch.

Gothic: The ecclesiastical architecture of the Middle Ages, traditionally classified as Early English, Decorated or Perpendicular.

Gothick: A term used to describe the fanciful adaptation of medieval architecture for domestic buildings during the late eighteenth and early nineteenth centuries.

Greek Revival: An architectural style very popular in the first years of the nineteenth century, developed from a scholarly interest in the earliest Greek buildings. It was characterised by austerity and an imposing dignity, and usually involved the use of the giant **portico** as a dominant feature. See also **Neo-classical**.

Headers: Bricks used with their length into the wall so that the ends show on the exterior.

Hipped roof: A roof with all four sides sloping.

Keystone: The central stone in an arch, usually wedge-shaped and larger than the rest. Often found above windows.

Lintel: A length of timber or stone placed across the top of an opening in the wall in order to support the section of wall above.

Modillions: Brackets resembling square blocks, set at close intervals under a **cornice** or **pediment**.

Neo-classical: A style which attempted to refine Palladianism by the study of authentic Greek rather than Roman architecture. A minority taste during the later years of the eighteenth century, it led to the popular **Greek Revival** movement early in the nineteenth century.

Nogging: Bricks used to fill the panels of a timber-framed house.

Ogee arch: A form of late-medieval arch which became a popular feature of 'Gothick' taste during the eighteenth century.

Orders: See end of Part Two.

Oriel window: See **Bay window**.

Palladian: A style of Renaissance architecture derived from classical Roman buildings. It was introduced into England by Inigo Jones, who had studied the versions of it produced by the Italian architect Palladio.

Parapet: A low wall guarding a drop. Used particularly on bridges and above the eaves of houses.

Pediment: A feature in the form of a shallow triangle, normally at the eaves or over a door or window. If the sloping sides do not meet at the apex it is called an open pediment. If the base line has a gap in the centre it is a broken pediment. A similar feature designed with curved lines is called a **segmental pediment.**

Piano nobile: The floor containing the main reception rooms of a house.

Picturesque: A school of taste that emerged in the second half of the eighteenth century, involving a highly romantic and often sentimental view of nature and art. In architecture it resulted in a spate of 'castles', thatched cottages, artificial ruins and other follies, as well as a passion for the type of landscaping which produced a series of carefully composed views.

Pilaster: A projecting vertical strip of stone or wood, conforming to the classical Orders and designed to give the effect of a square column sunk into the wall. The term 'giant pilaster' is used when the feature extends to the full height of a façade. A 'pilaster strip' is a similar feature (often in brick) with no classical embellishment.

Portico: An impressive entrance porch usually comprising a **pediment** supported on a row of columns. A 'giant portico' extends the full height of the façade.

Quoins: The dressed stones reinforcing the external corners of a brick or stone building. They often project from the wall surface, in which case they are known as rusticated quoins.

Random stonework: A stone-laying technique where no attempt is made to lay the stones in courses.

Reredos: A decorative screen behind the altar in a church.

Round-headed: See **Segment-headed**.

Rubble masonry: Building stones varying in size and often only roughly faced. Rubble masonry laid in approximately regular lines is 'coursed rubble'.

Rustication: The practice of cutting grooves between stones in ashlar work to create the appearance of neat mortar joints. If only the horizontal joints are cut it is known as banded rustication. The term is sometimes applied to the technique of cutting grooves or holes on the surface of dressed stone as a form of decoration. See also **Quoins**.

Segment-headed: Used of doors or windows slightly curved at the top. In **round-headed** windows or doors the curve is semi-circular.

Segmental pediment: See **Pediment**.

Stretchers: Bricks laid so that their long sides appear on the exterior.

String course: A projecting moulding on the façade of a house, forming a horizontal dividing line between storeys.

Venetian window: A window consisting of a central round-headed section with lower and narrower sections on each side, a typical Palladian feature.

Voussoir: A wedge-shaped stone or brick used in an arch.

Bibliography

Addison, Sir William, *Local Styles of the English Parish Church*, Batsford (1982)

Armstrong, J. R., *Traditional Buildings Accessible to the Public*, EP Publishing (1979)

Barley, M. W.,
The English Farmhouse and Cottage, Routledge and Kegan Paul (1961)
The House and Home, Vista Books (1963)

Blackwall, A., *Historic Bridges of Shropshire*, Shropshire Libraries (1985)

Braun, H., *Elements of English Architecture*, David & Charles (1973)

Briggs, Martin, *The English Farmhouse*, Batsford (1953)

Brook, F., *The Industrial Archaeology of the British Isles — West Midlands*, Batsford (1977)

Brown, J. J., *The Mines of Shropshire*, Moorland Publishing (1976)

Brown, R. J.,
The English Country Cottage, Robert Hale (1979)
English Farmhouses, Robert Hale (1982)

Brunskill, R. and Clifton-Taylor, A., *English Brickwork*, Ward Lock (1977)

Cave, Lyndon F., *The Smaller English House*, Robert Hale (1981)

Clifton-Taylor, Alec, *The Pattern of English Building*, Faber (1972)

Cruickshank, D., *A Guide to the Georgian Buildings of Britain and Ireland*, Weidenfeld and Nicholson (1985)

Cunnington, Pamela, *How Old is Your House?* Alphabooks (1980)

Furneaux Jordan, R., *A Concise History of Western Architecture*, Thames & Hudson (1969)

Girouard, Mark, *Life in the English Country House*, Yale University Press (1978)

Hadfield, Charles, *Canals of the West Midlands*, David & Charles (1985)

Muir, Richard,
The English Village, Thames & Hudson (1980)
The Shell Guide to Reading the Landscape, Michael Joseph (1981)
The Stones of Britain, Michael Joseph (1986)

Muter, W. G., *The Buildings of an Industrial Community*, Phillimore (1979)

Nye, Thelma, *Parish Church Architecture*, Batsford (1965)

Penoyre, J. and J., *Houses in the Landscape*, Faber (1978)

Pevsner, N., *Buildings of England: Shropshire*, Penguin Books (1958)

Reed, Michael, *The Georgian Triumph 1700-1830*, Paladin Books (1983)

Robinson, J. M., *The Architecture of Northern England*, Macmillan (1986)

Royal Commission on Historical Monuments, *Nonconformist Chapels and Meeting Houses — Shropshire and Staffordshire*, (1986)

Trinder, B.,
The Making of the Industrial Landscape, Dent (1982)
Coalbrookdale, Ironbridge Gorge Museum Trust (1979)

Various authors, *Spirit of the Age*, BBC (1975)

Index